BACK TO THE FUTURE

THE OFFICIAL COLORING BOOK

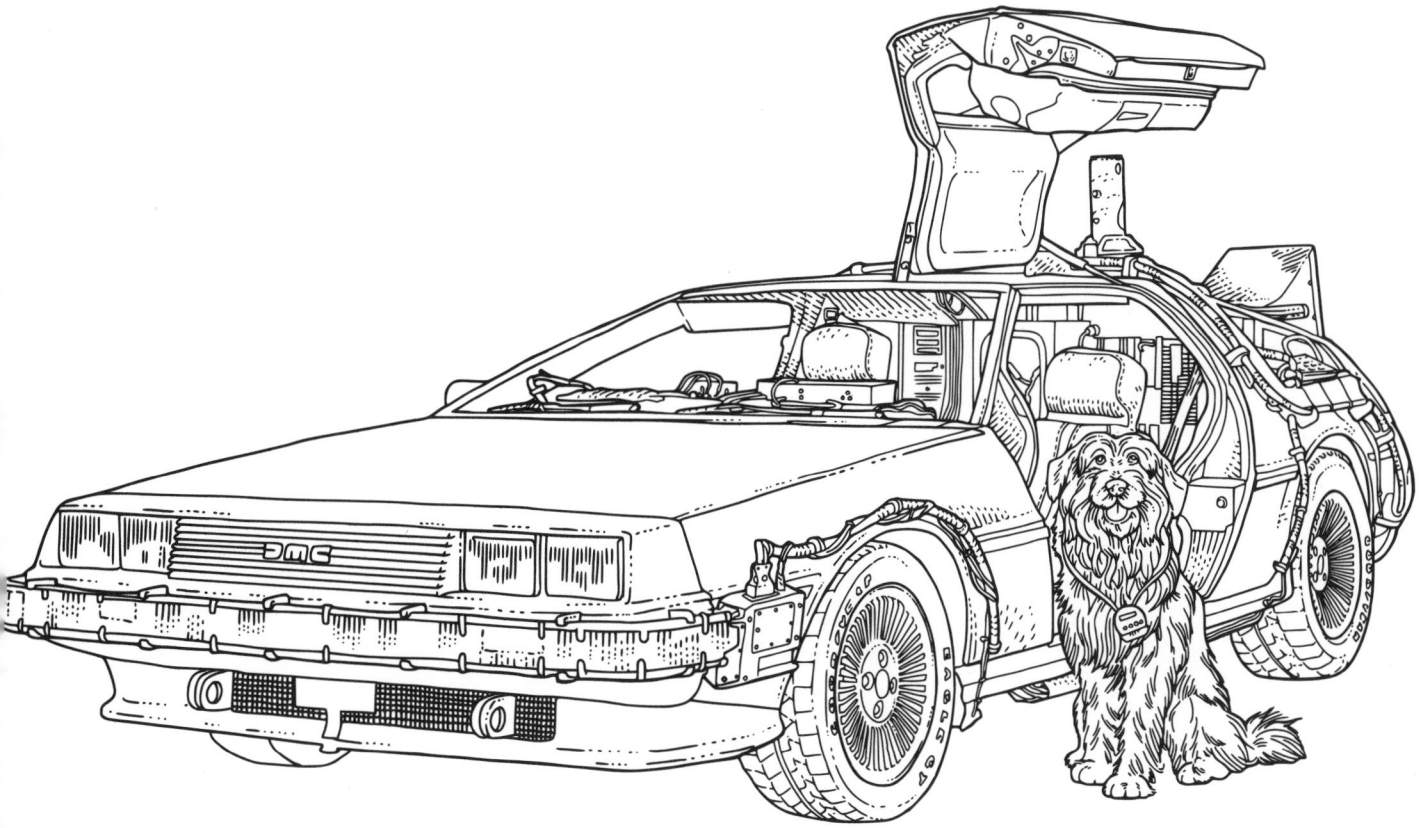

T0053671

INSIGHT
EDITIONS

SAN RAFAEL • LOS ANGELES • LONDON

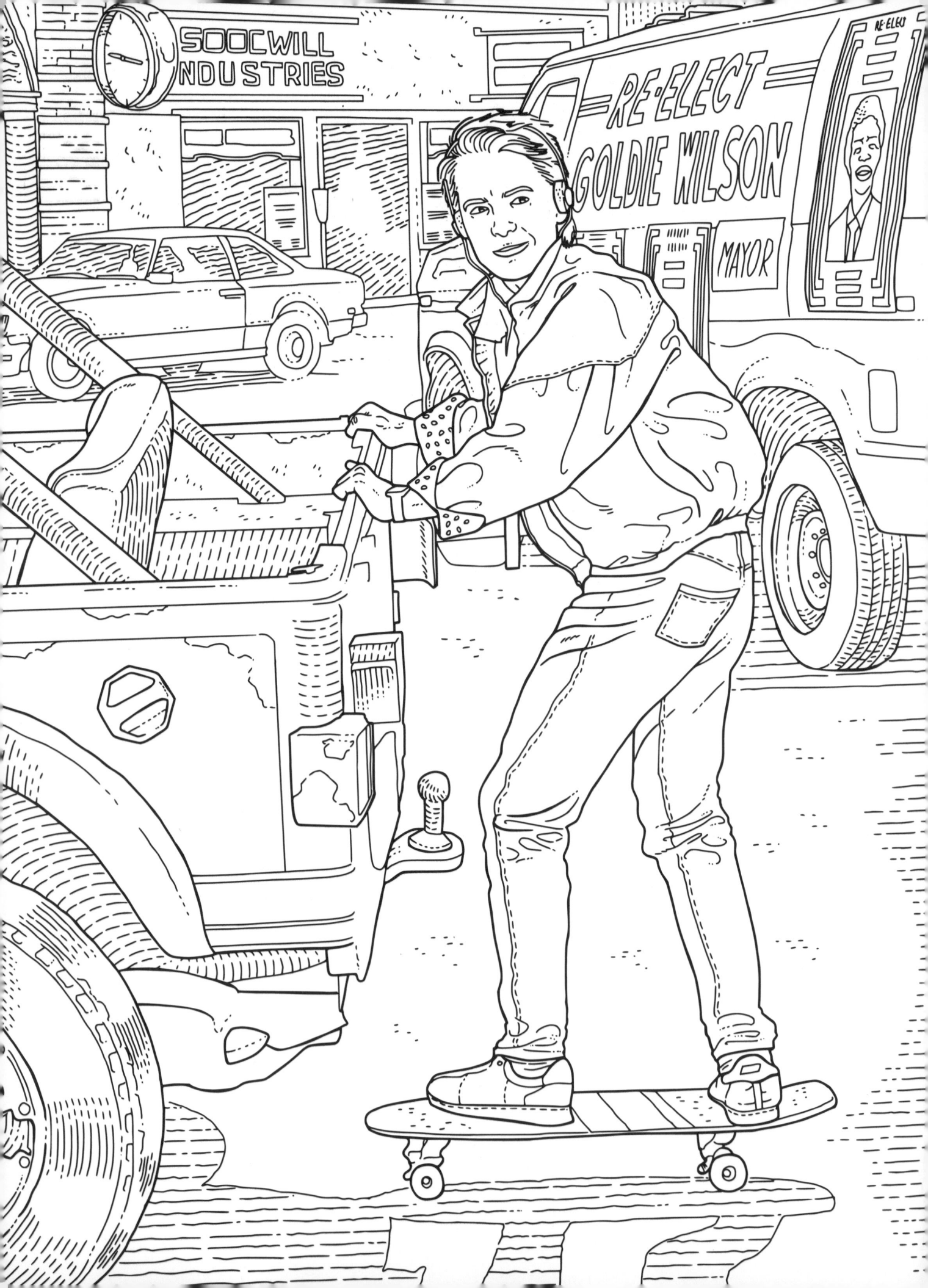
SOOCWILL
NDUSTRIES
RE-ELECT
GOLDIE WILSON
MAYOR
RE-ELECT

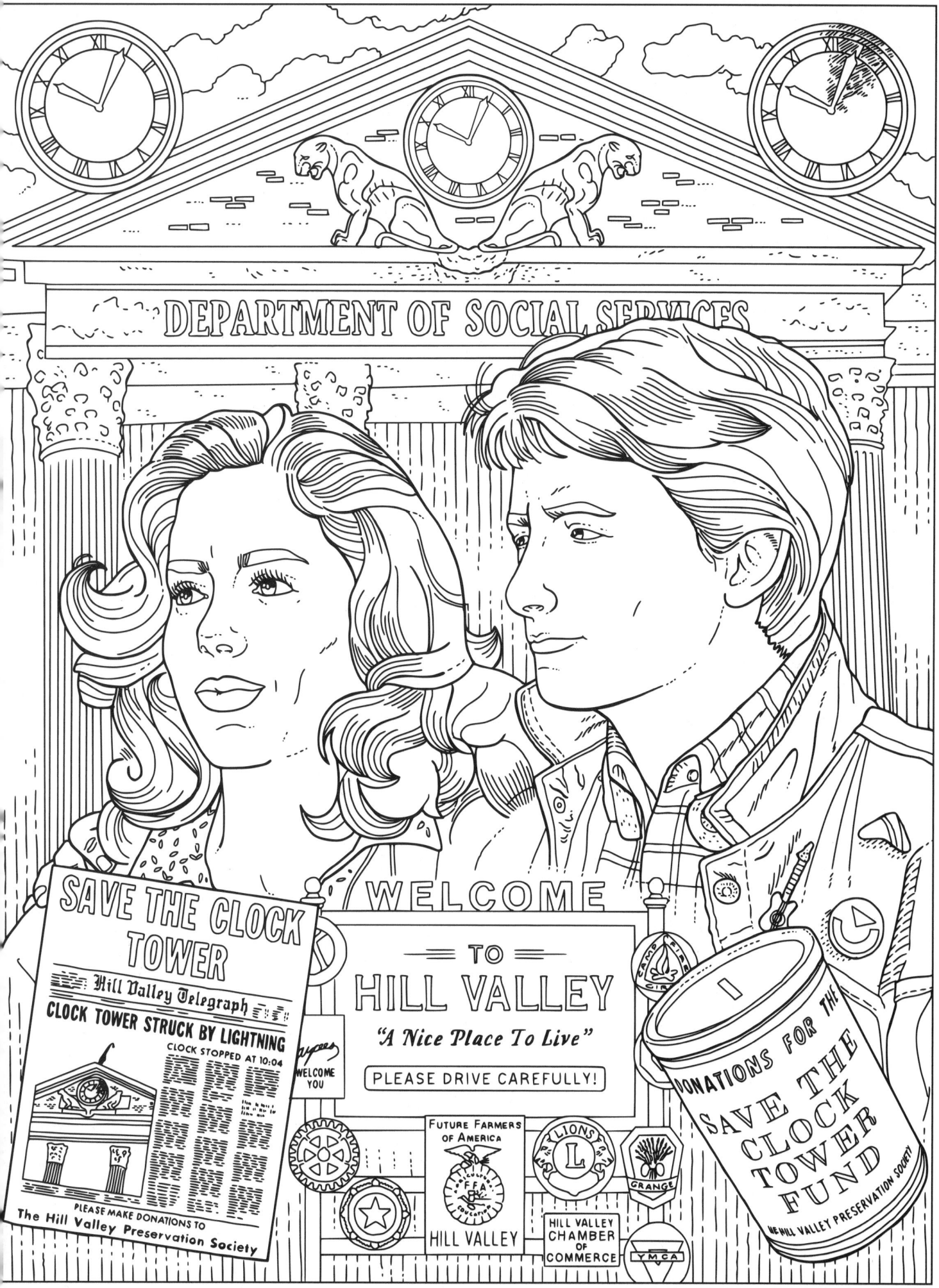
DEPARTMENT OF SOCIAL SERVICES
WELCOME
TO
HILL VALLEY
"A Nice Place To Live"
PLEASE DRIVE CAREFULLY!
WELCOME YOU
SAVE THE CLOCK TOWER
Hill Valley Telegraph
CLOCK TOWER STRUCK BY LIGHTNING
CLOCK STOPPED AT 10:04
PLEASE MAKE DONATIONS TO
The Hill Valley Preservation Society
DONATIONS FOR THE
SAVE THE CLOCK TOWER FUND
THE HILL VALLEY PRESERVATION SOCIETY
FUTURE FARMERS OF AMERICA
FFA
HILL VALLEY
LIONS
HILL VALLEY CHAMBER OF COMMERCE
GRANGE
YMCA

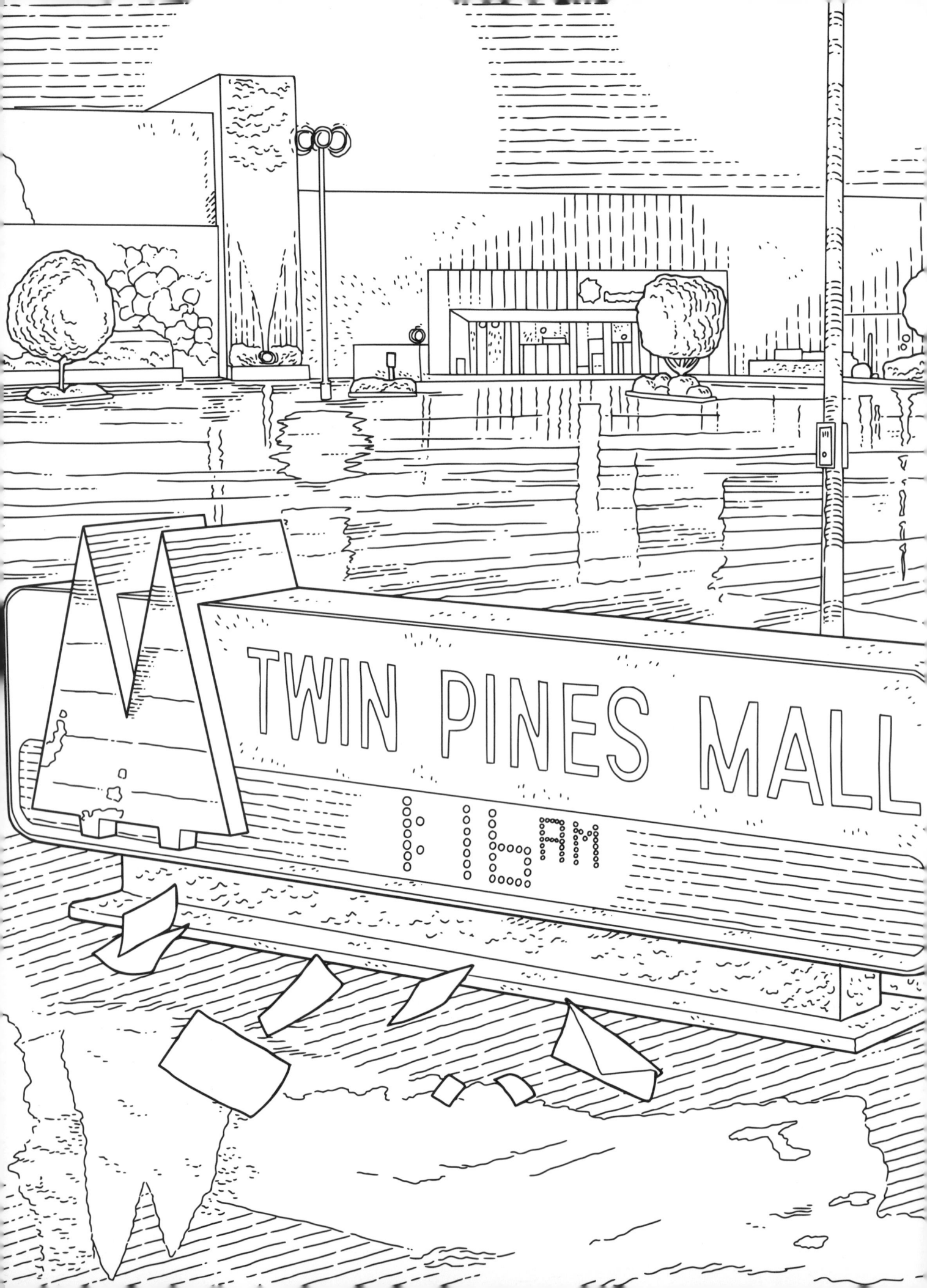
TWIN PINES MALL
6:15AM

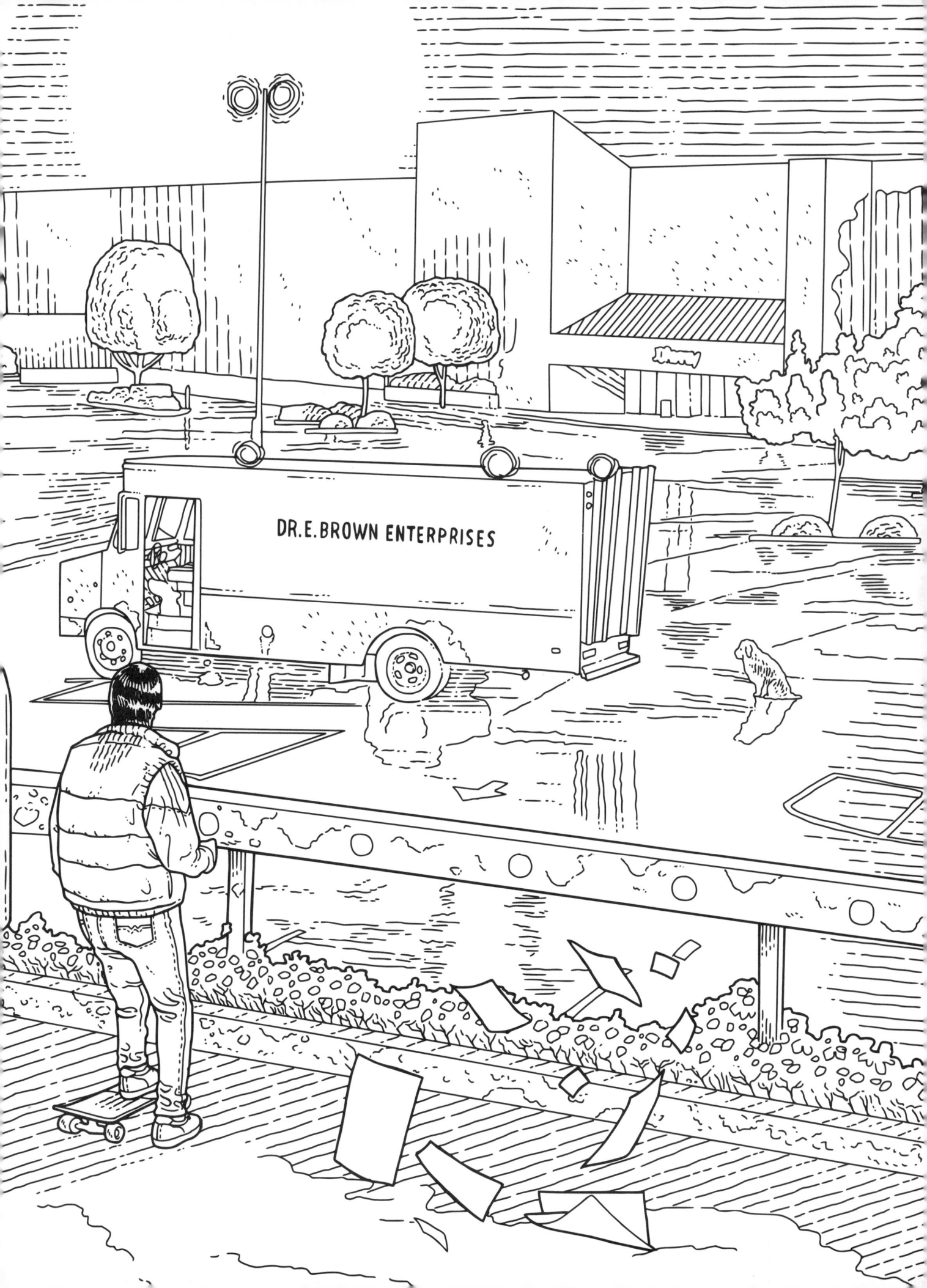
DR.E.BROWN ENTERPRISES

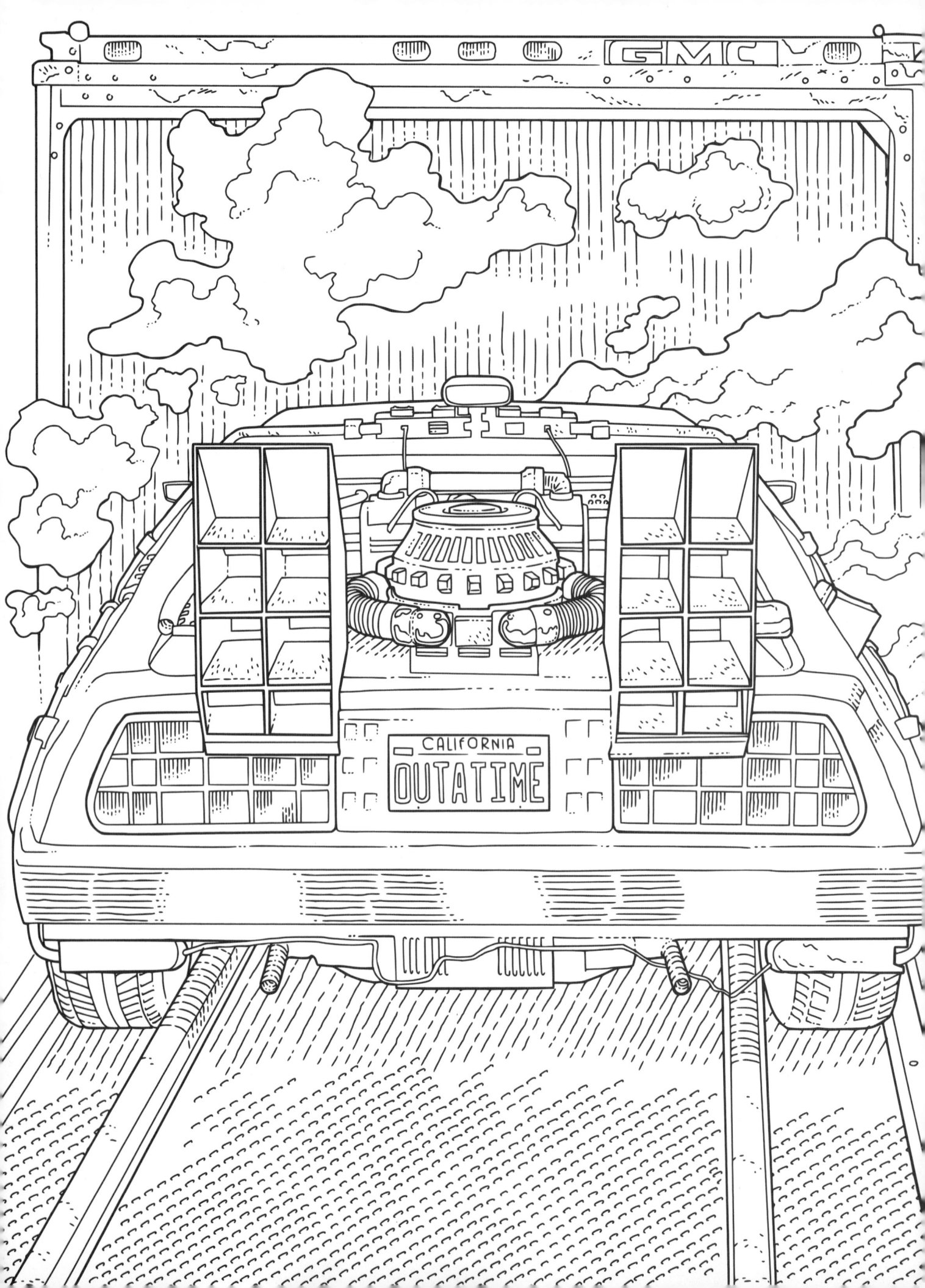
GMC
CALIFORNIA
OUTATIME

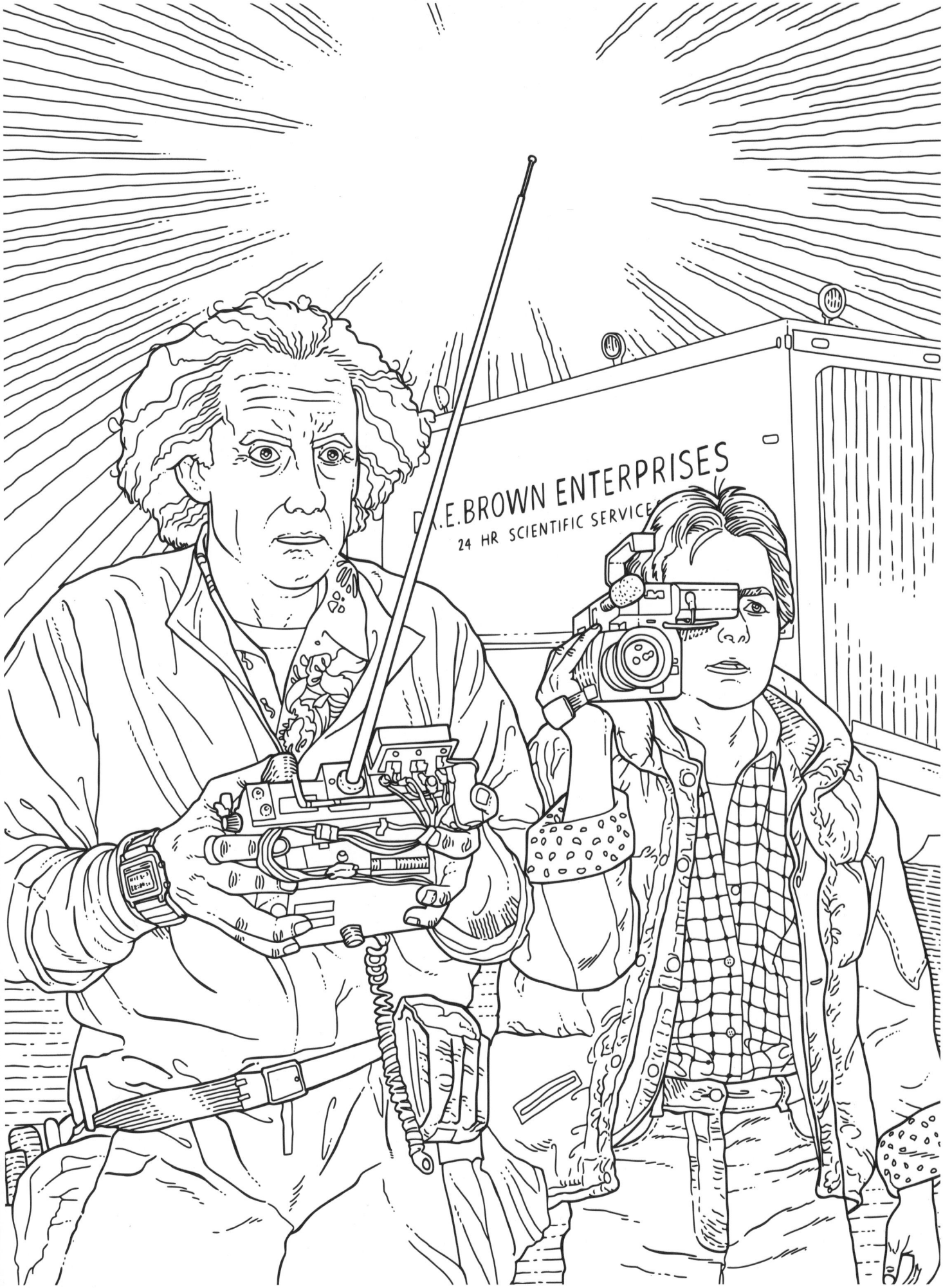
D.E.BROWN ENTERPRISES
24 HR SCIENTIFIC SERVICE

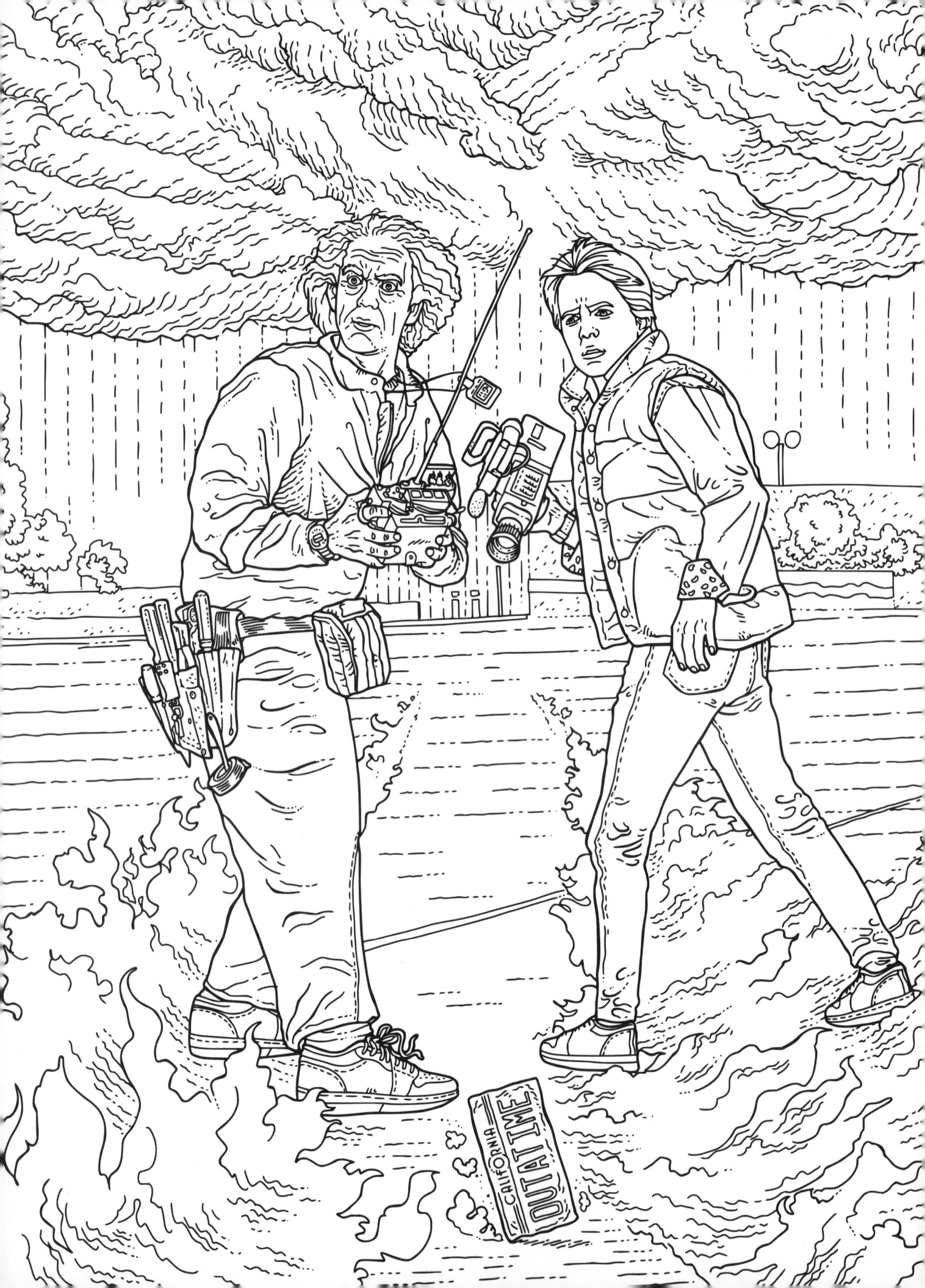
CALIFORNIA
OUTATIME

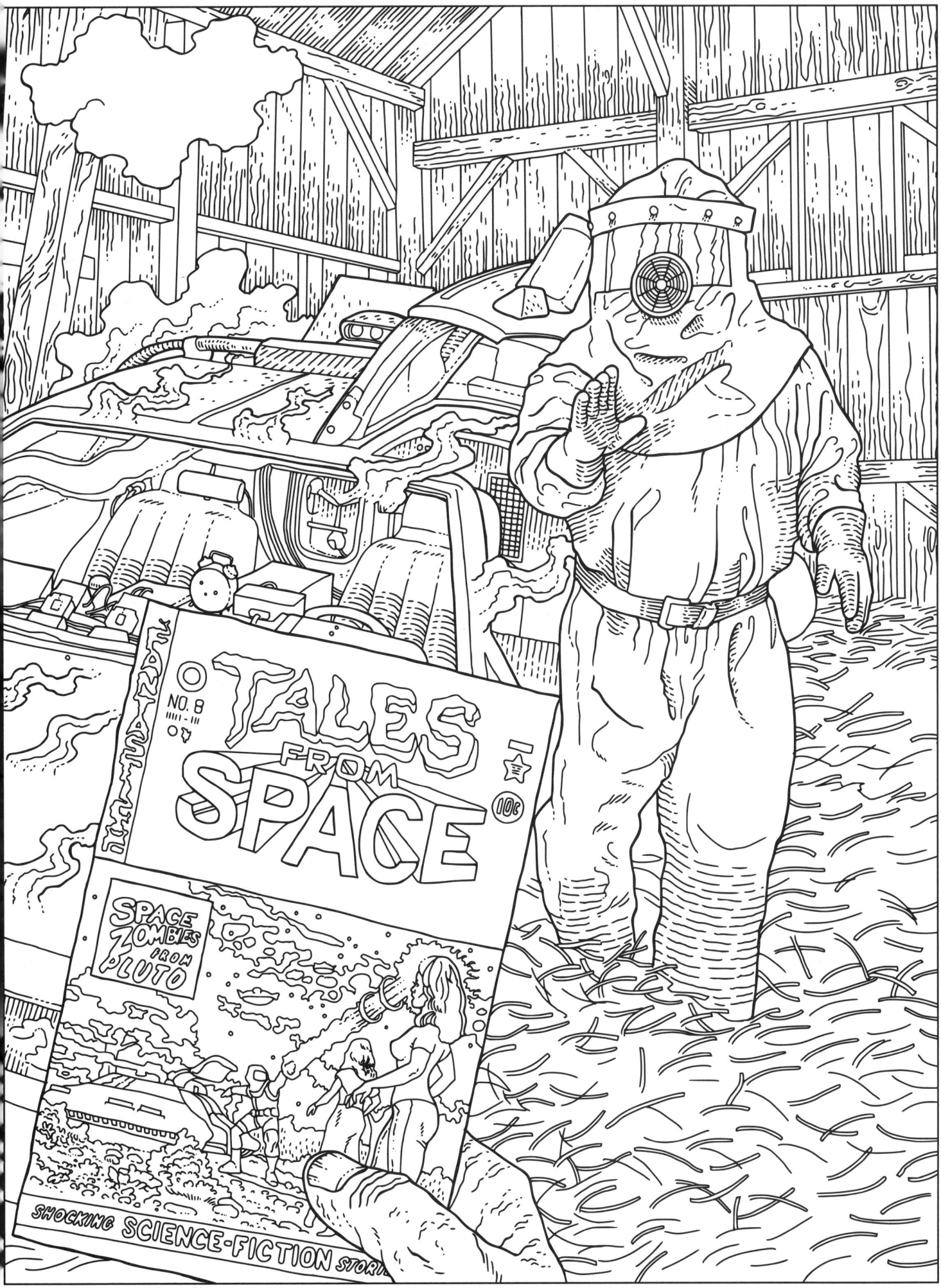
NO. 8
TALES FROM SPACE
10¢
SPACE ZOMBIES FROM PLUTO
SHOCKING SCIENCE-FICTION

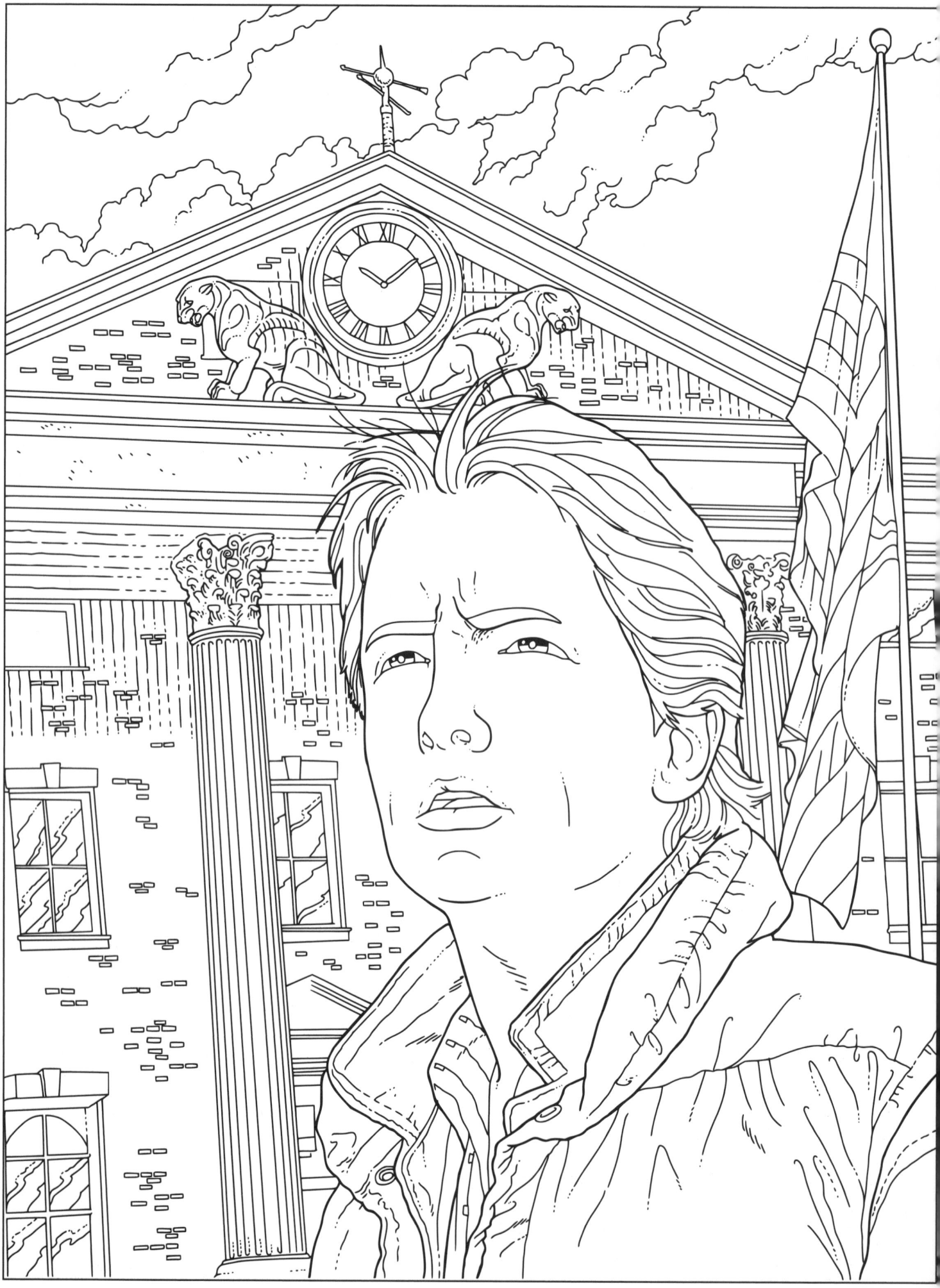

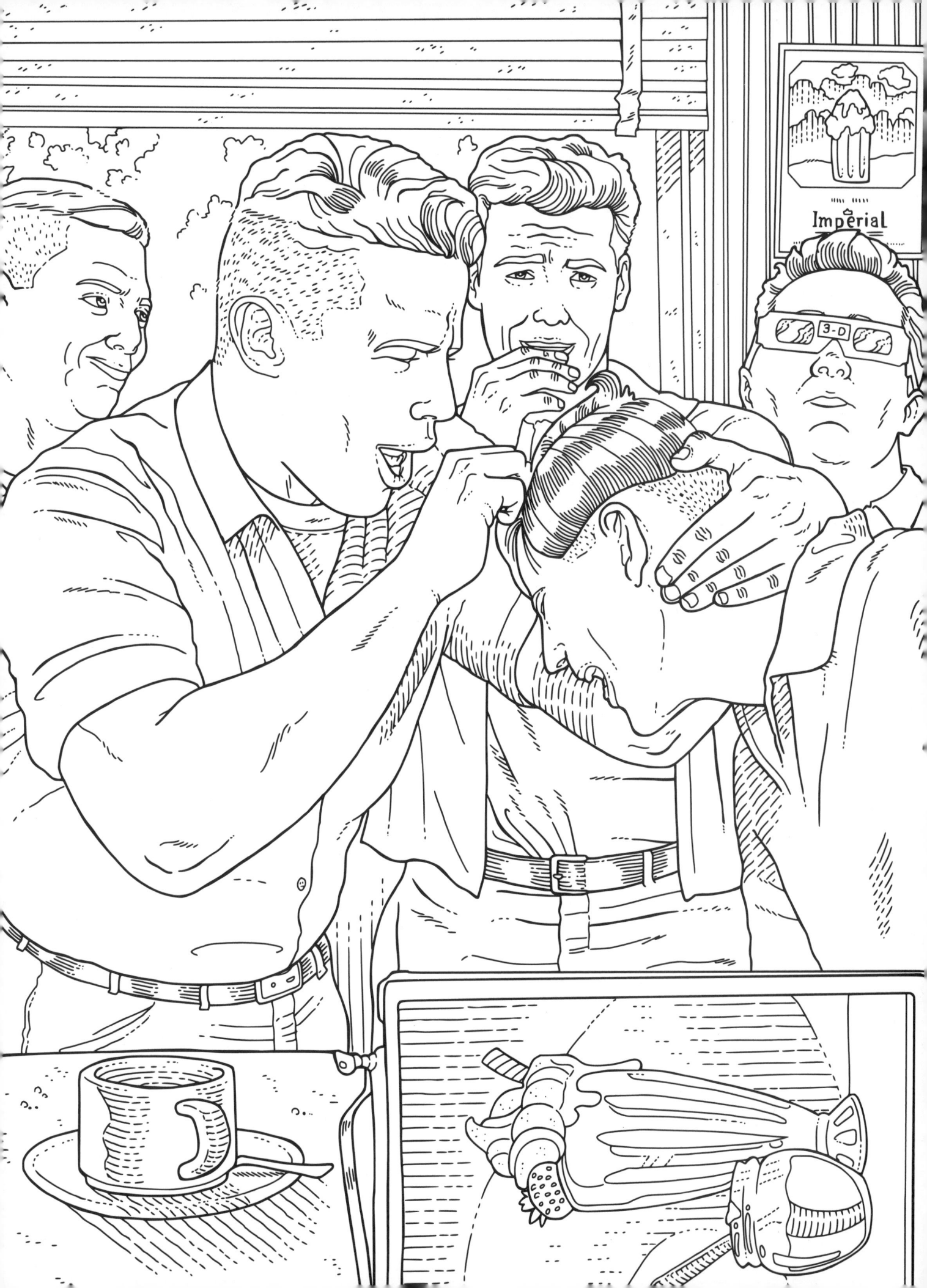
Impêrial
3-D

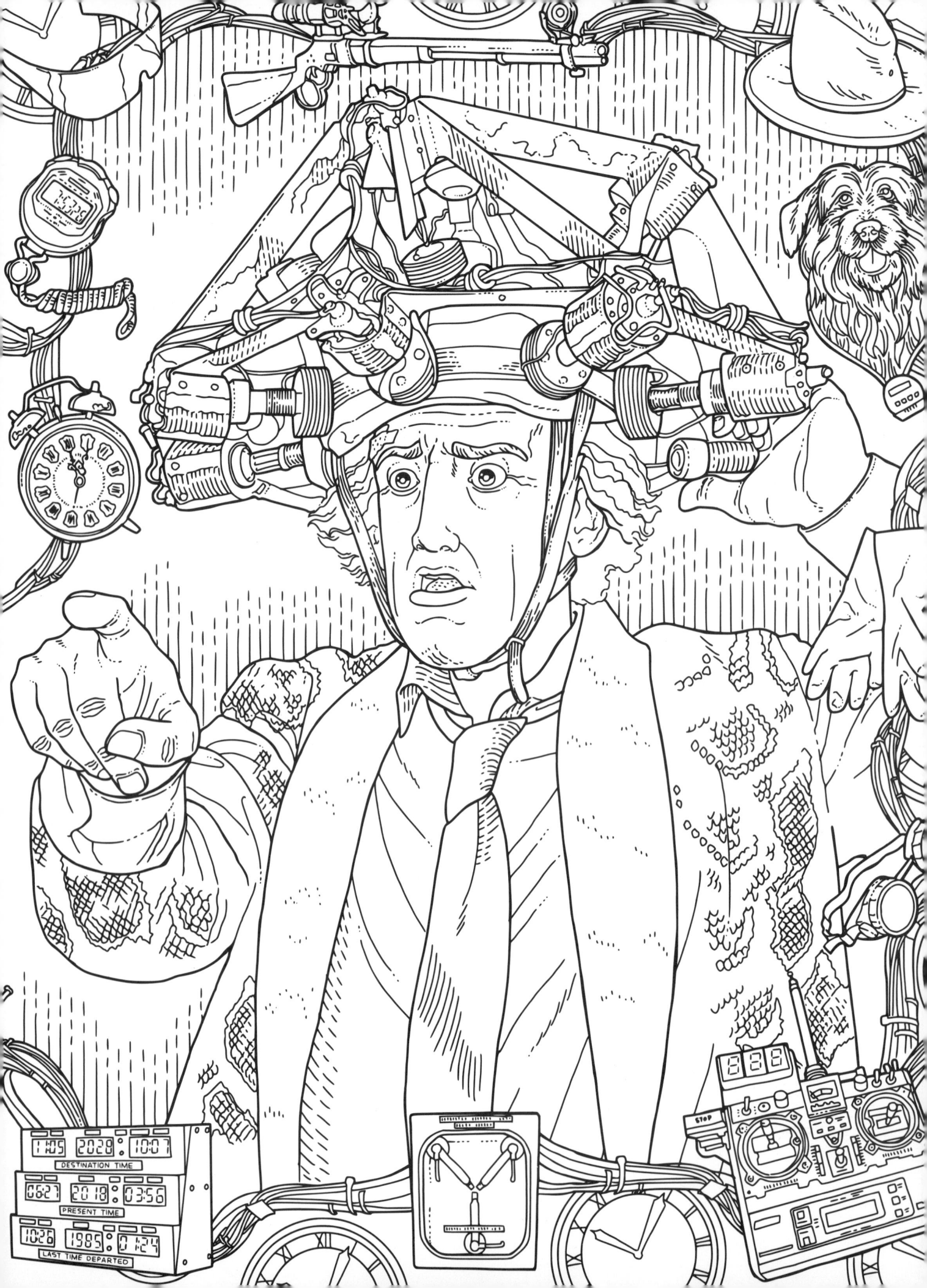
DESTINATION TIME
PRESENT TIME
LAST TIME DEPARTED
STOP

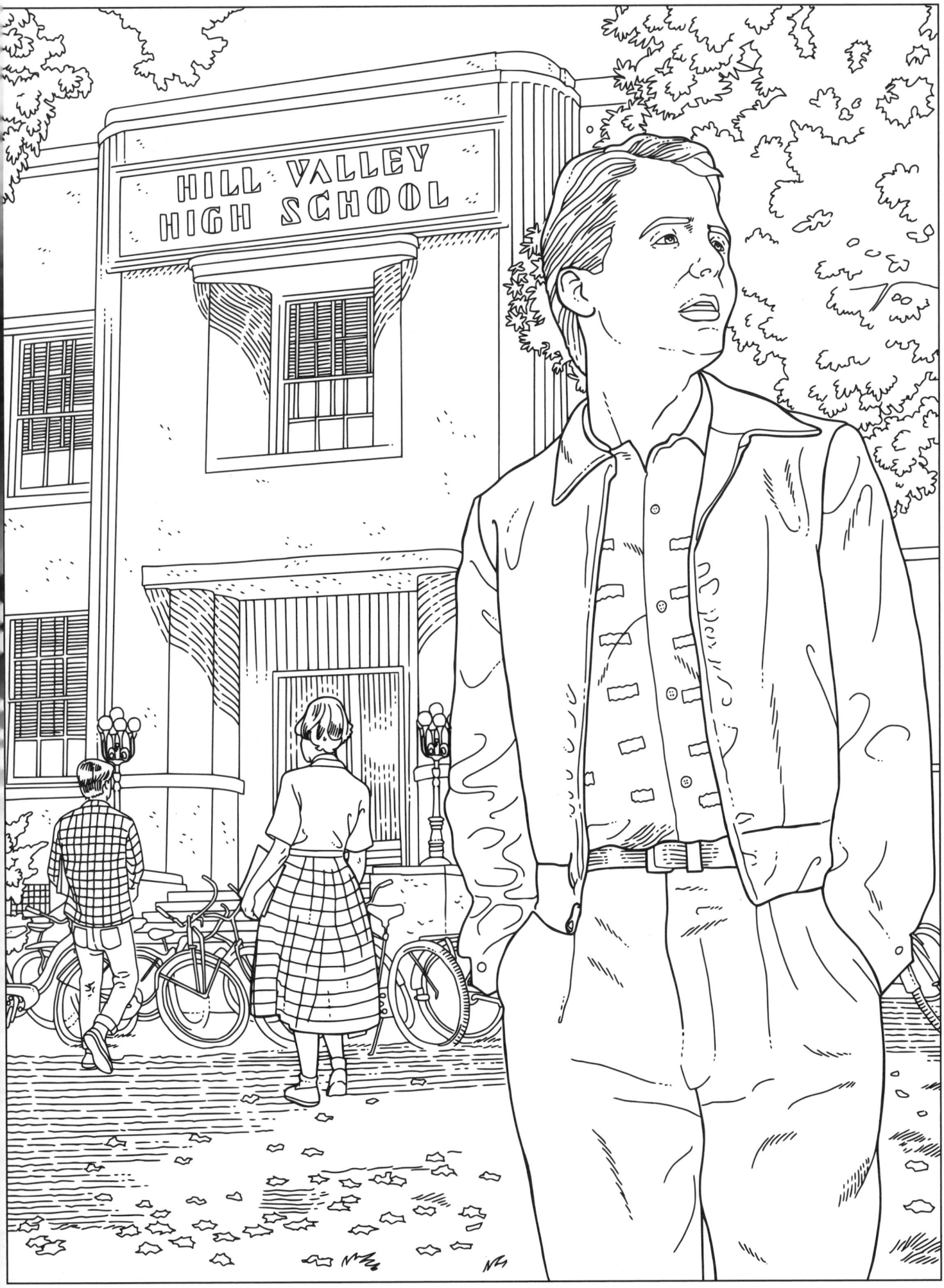
HILL VALLEY
HIGH SCHOOL

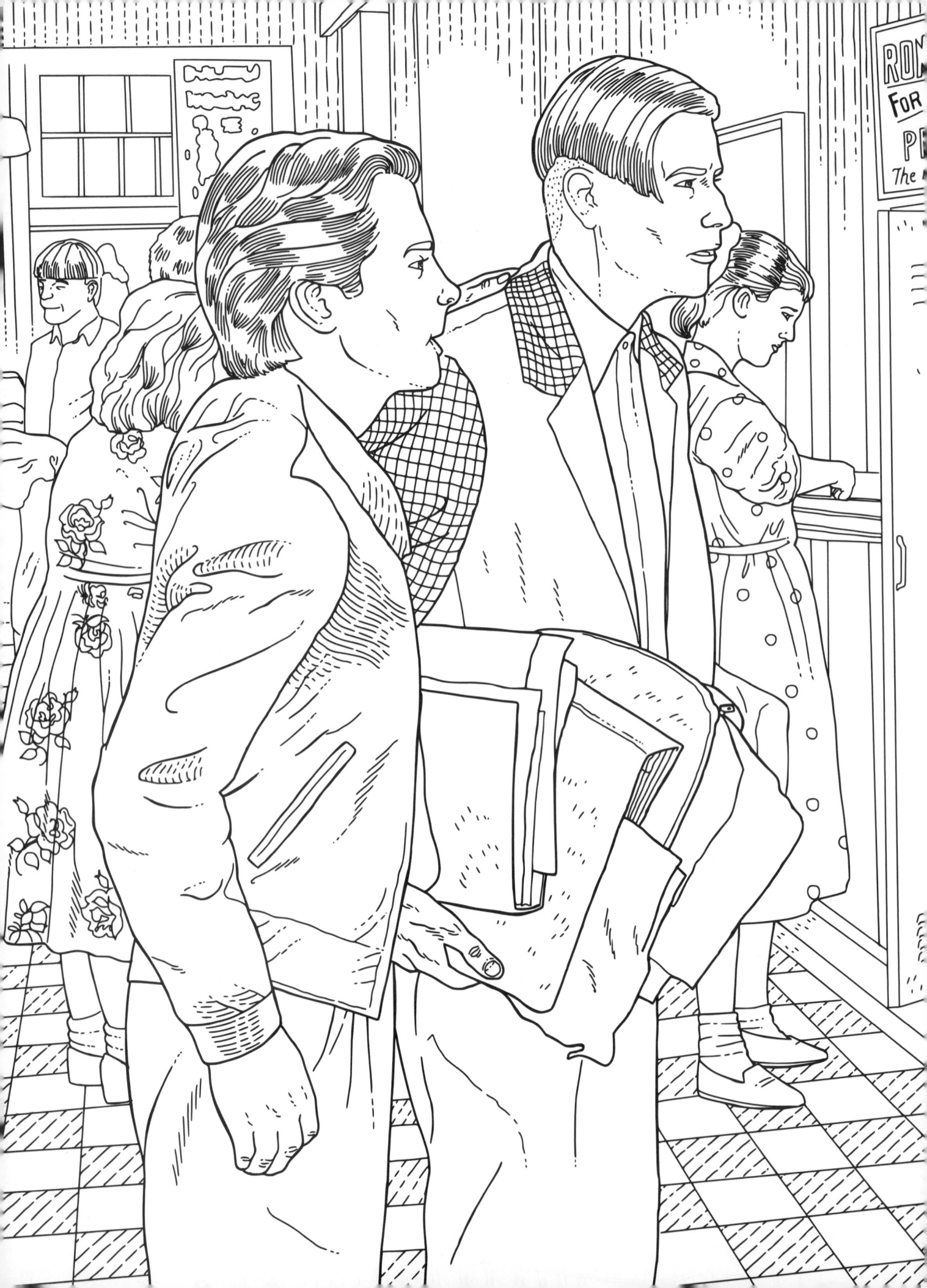
FOR
The

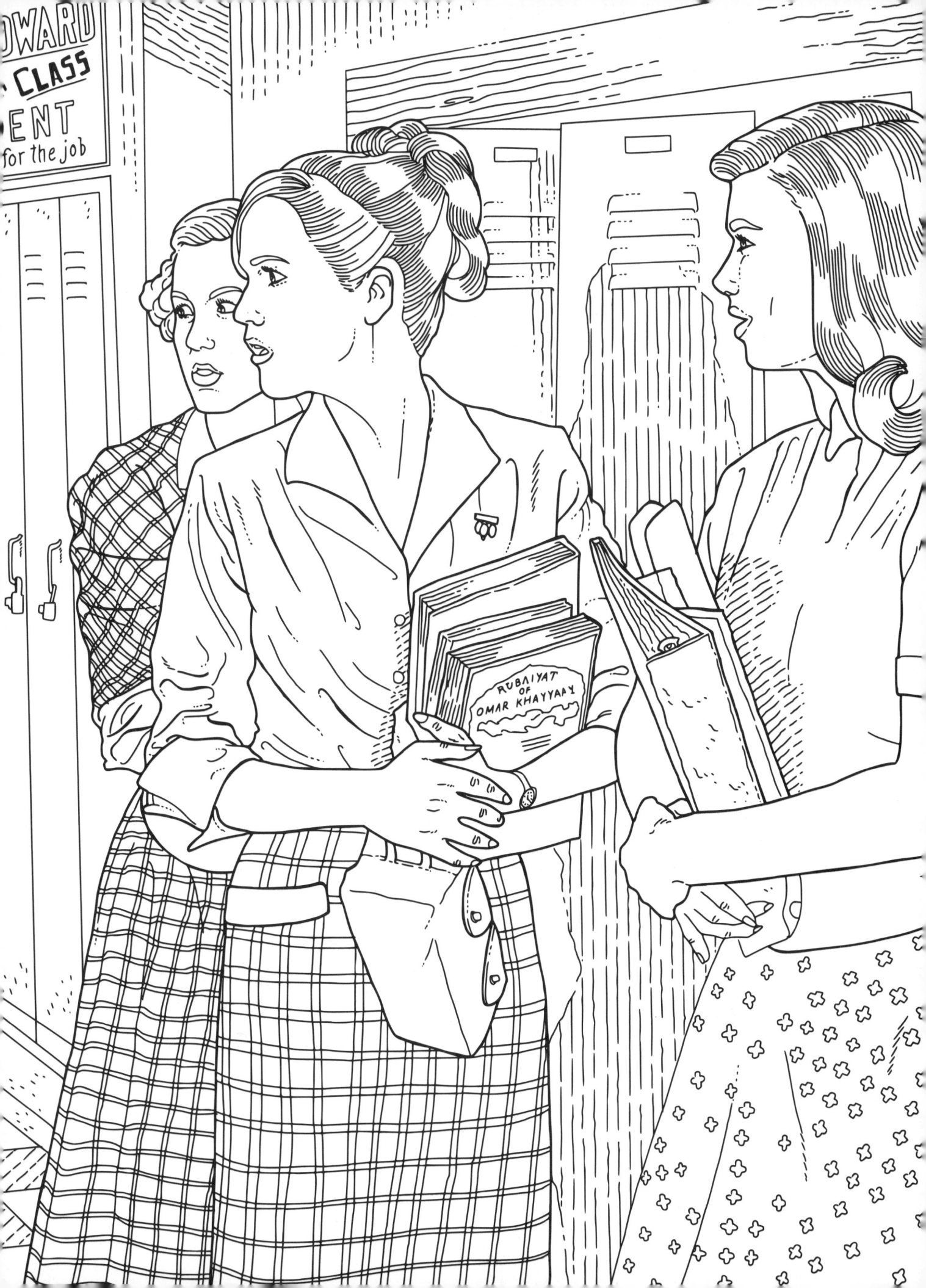
DWARD
CLASS
ENT
for the job
RUBAIYAT
OF
OMAR KHAYYAM

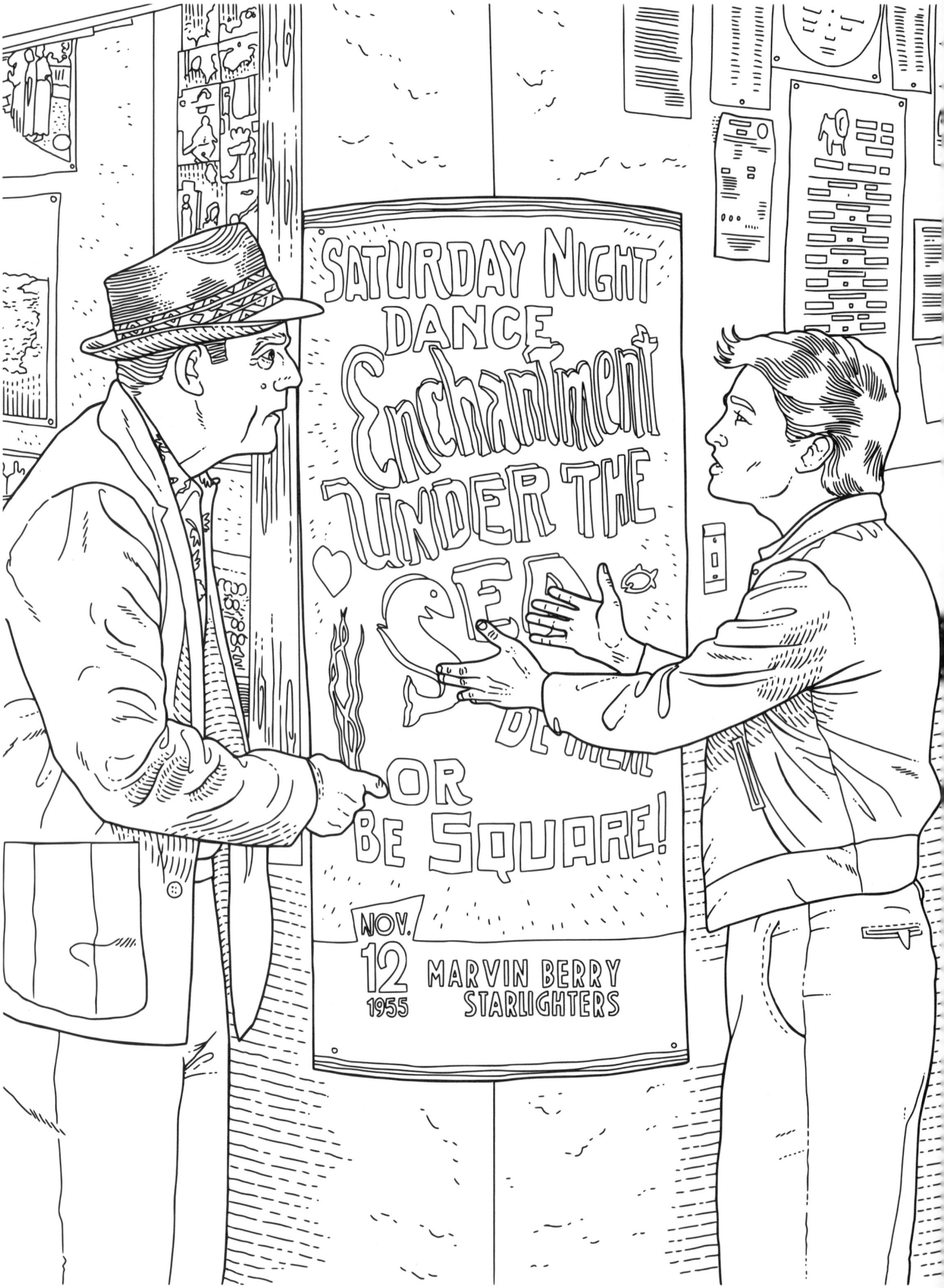
SATURDAY NIGHT
DANCE
Enchantment
UNDER THE
SEA
OR
BE SQUARE!
NOV.
12
1955
MARVIN BERRY
STARLIGHTERS

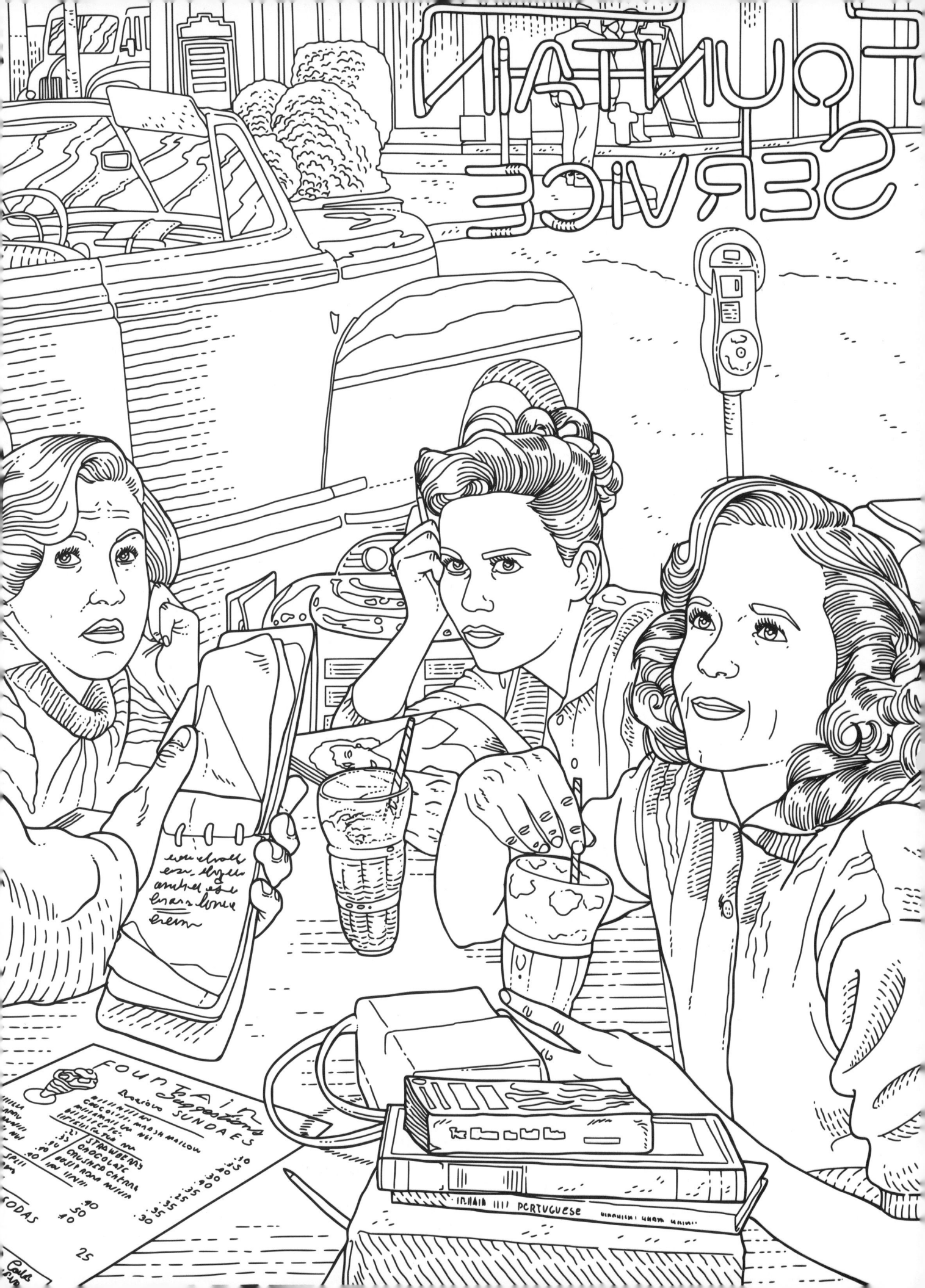
FOUNTAIN SERVICE
FOUNTAIN Suggestions
Various SUNDAES
STRAWBERRY
CHOCOLATE
CRUSHED CHERRY
PORTUGUESE

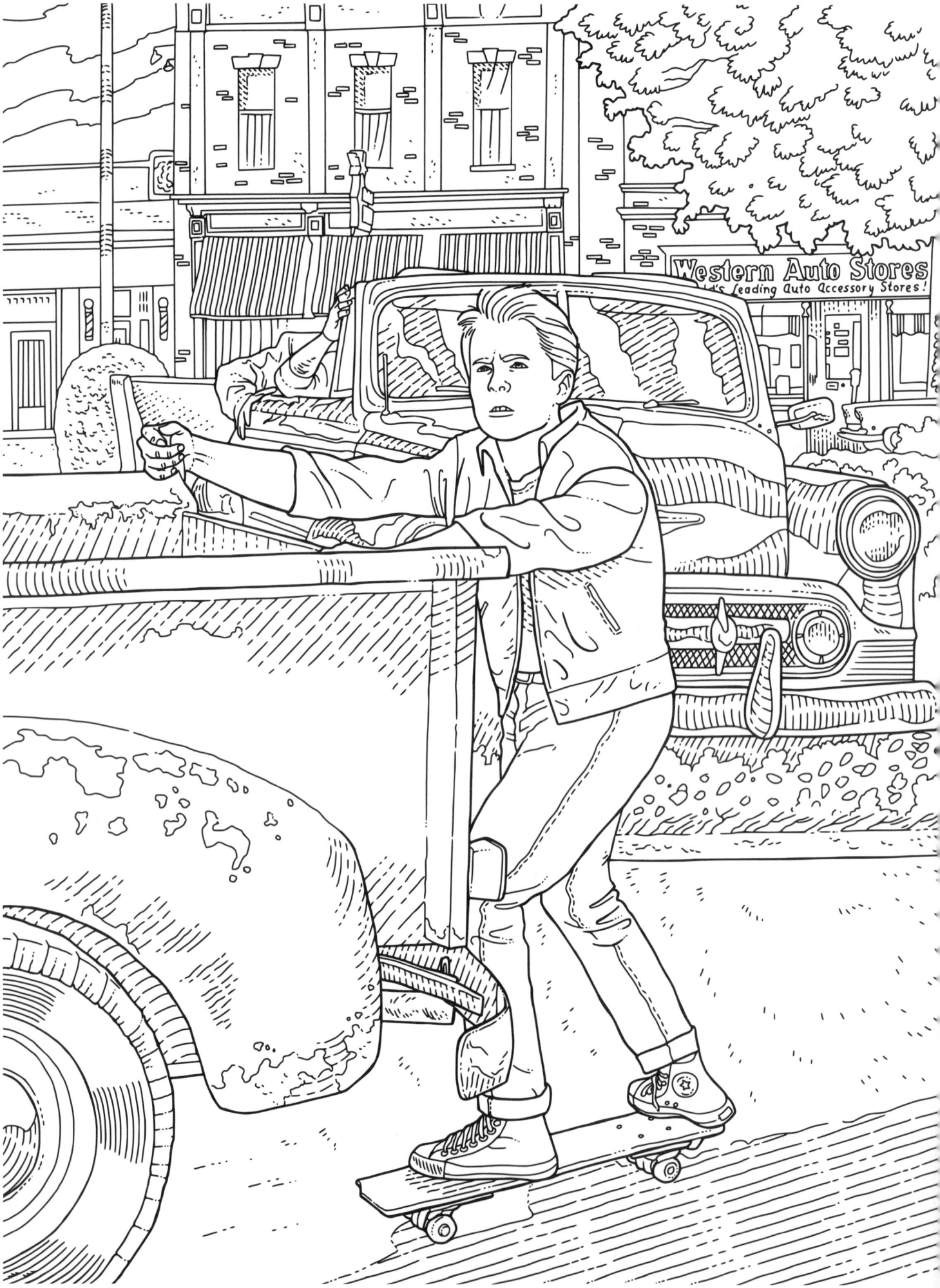
Western Auto Stores
d's Leading Auto Accessory Stores!

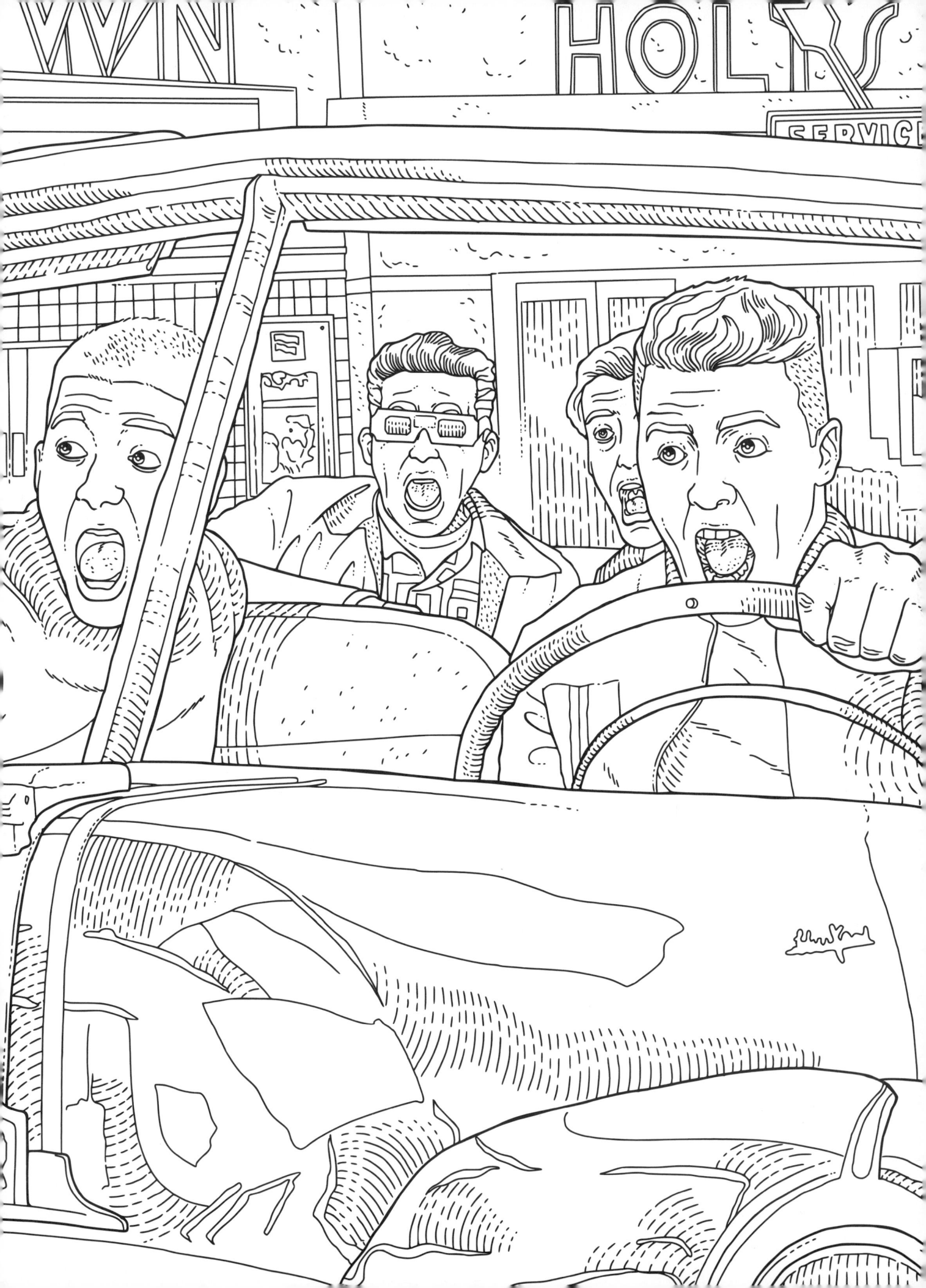
HOLLY
SERVICE

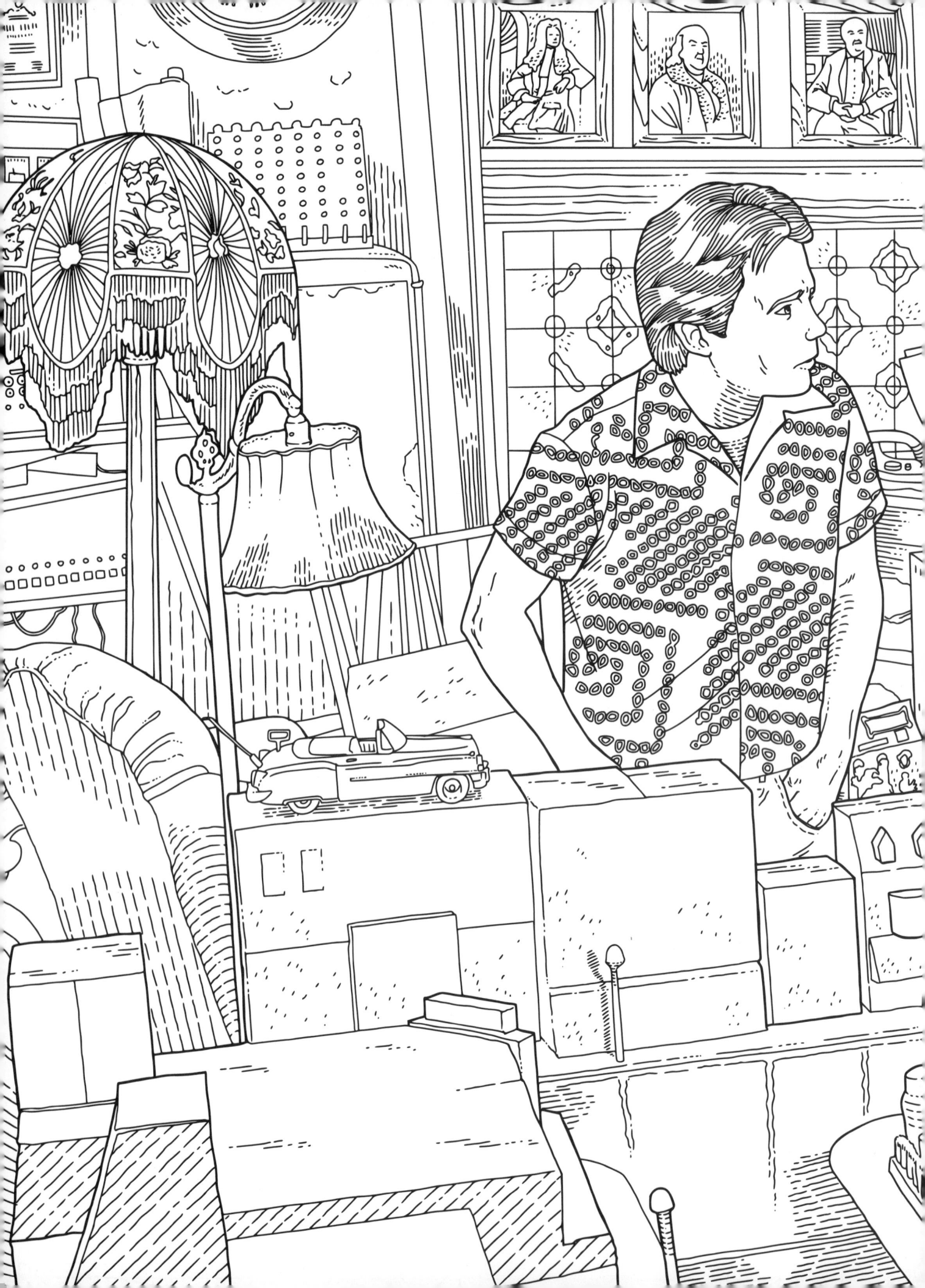

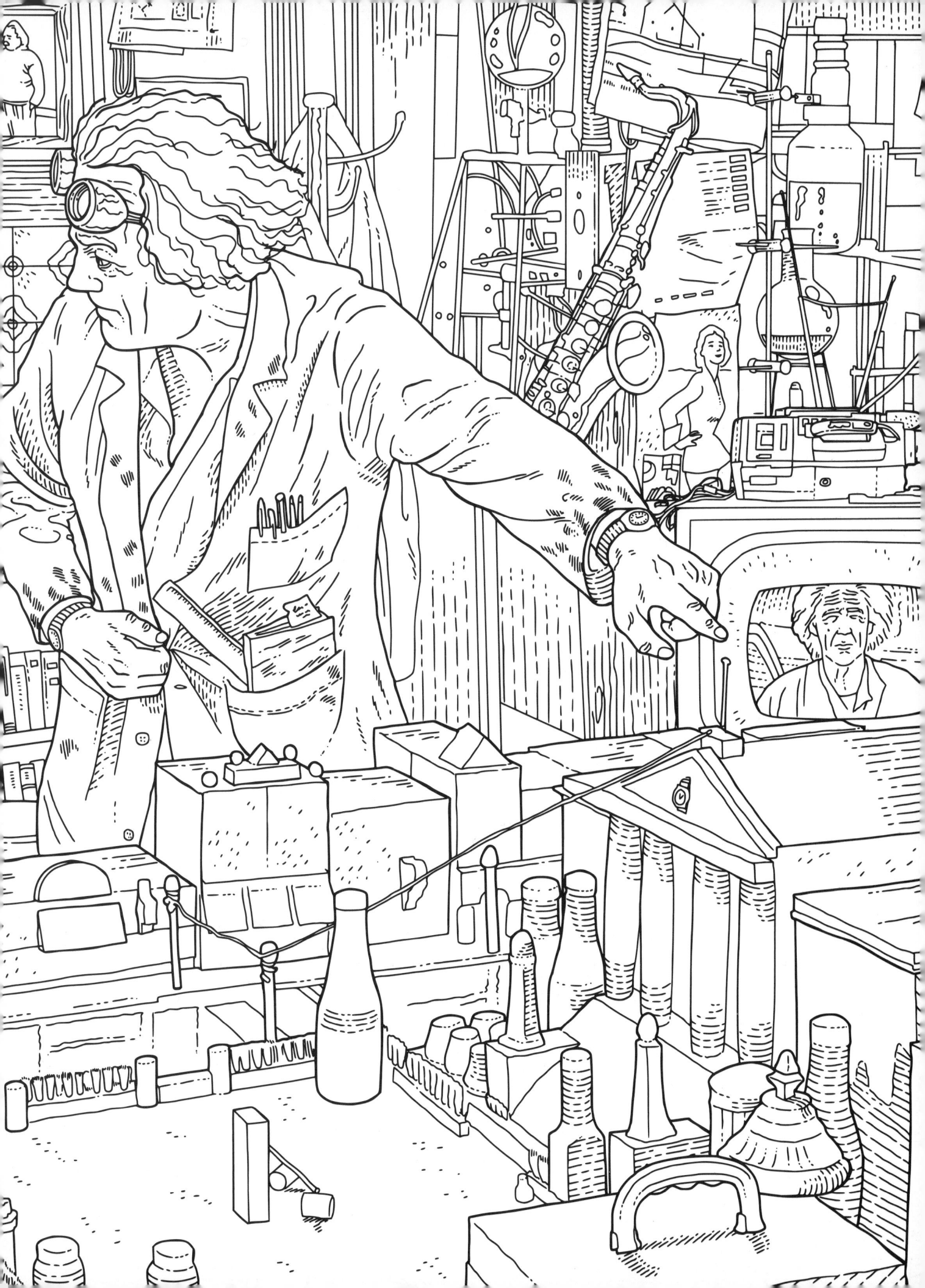

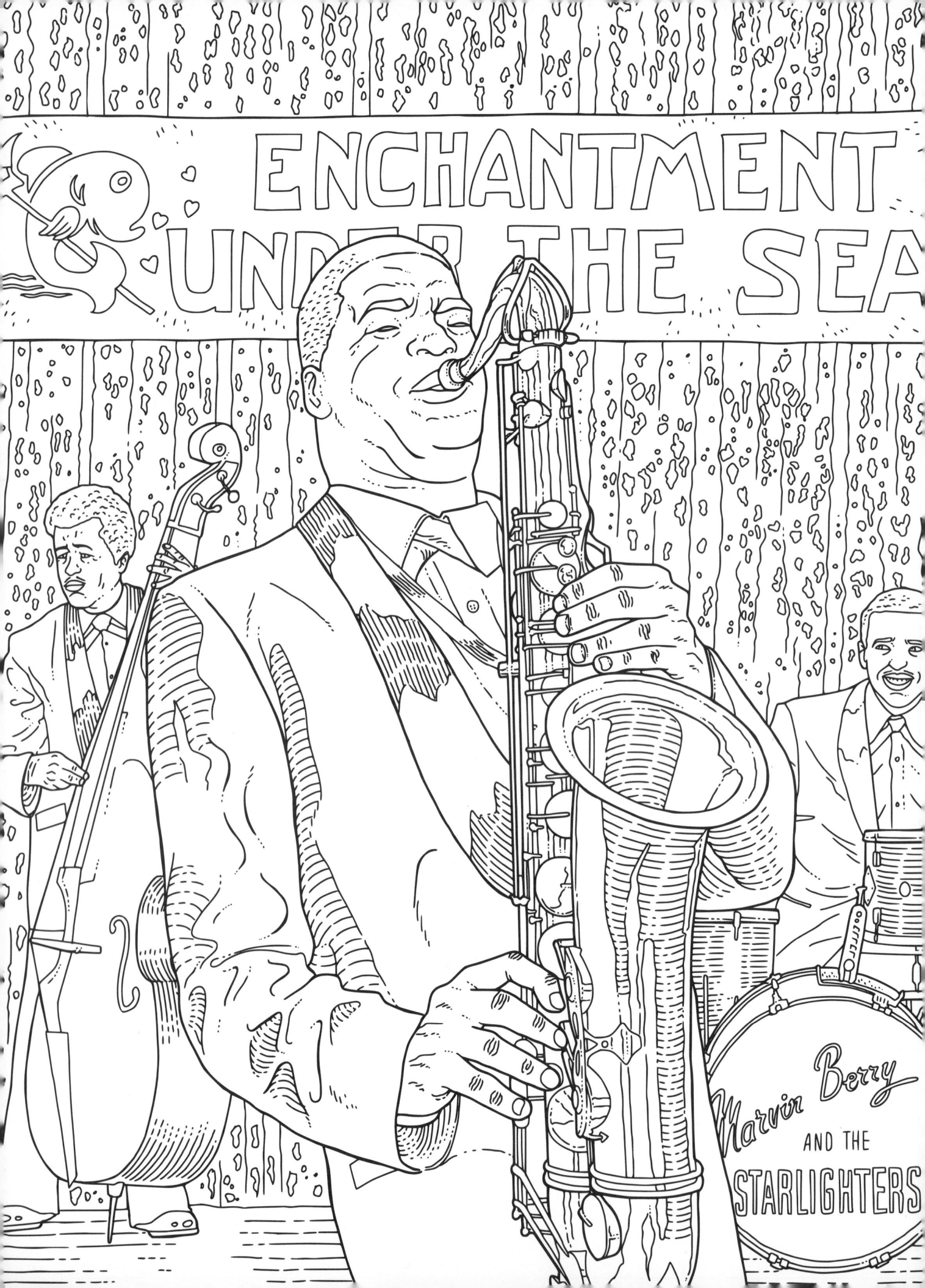
ENCHANTMENT
UNDER THE SEA
Marvin Berry
AND THE
STARLIGHTERS

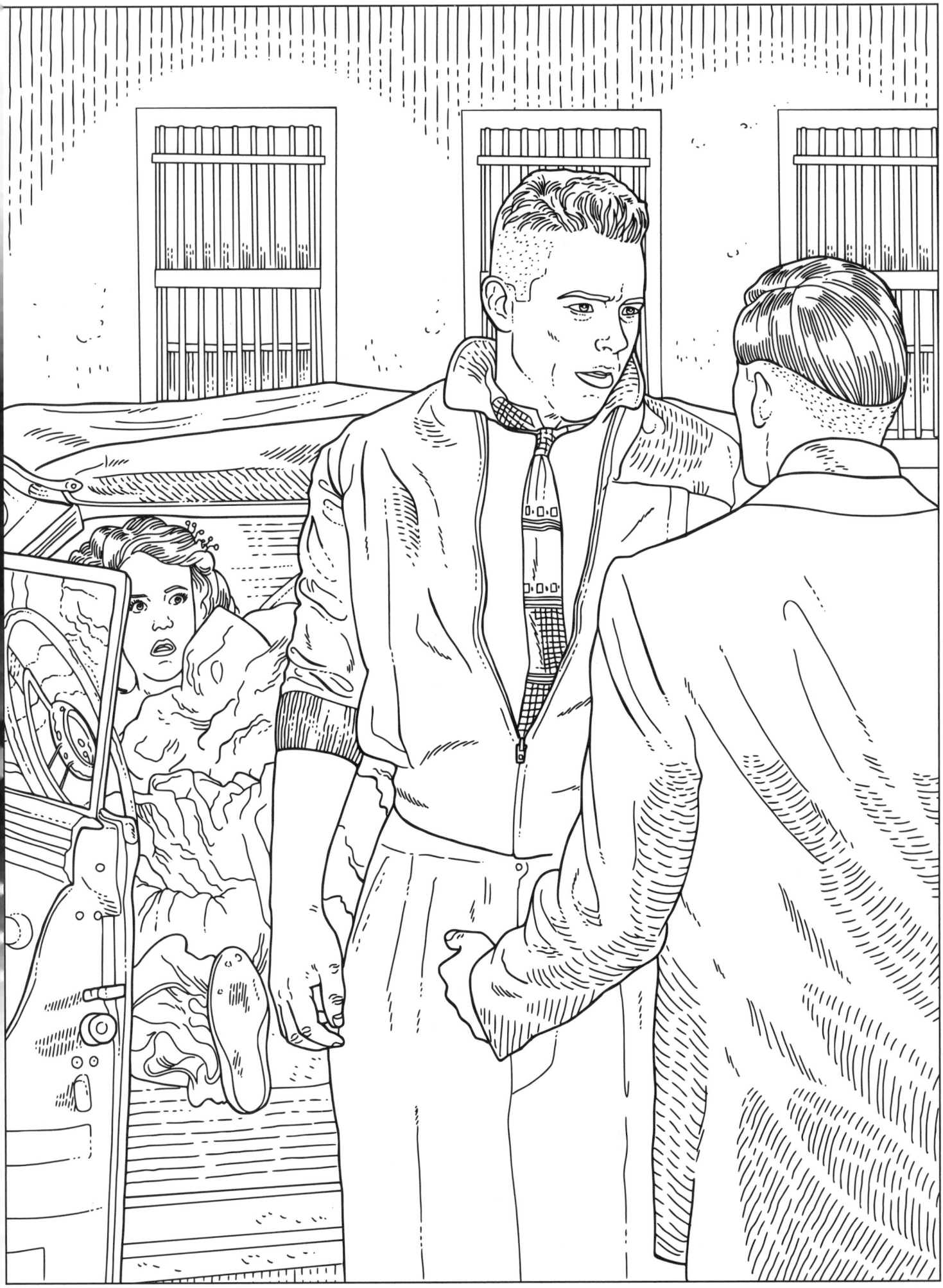

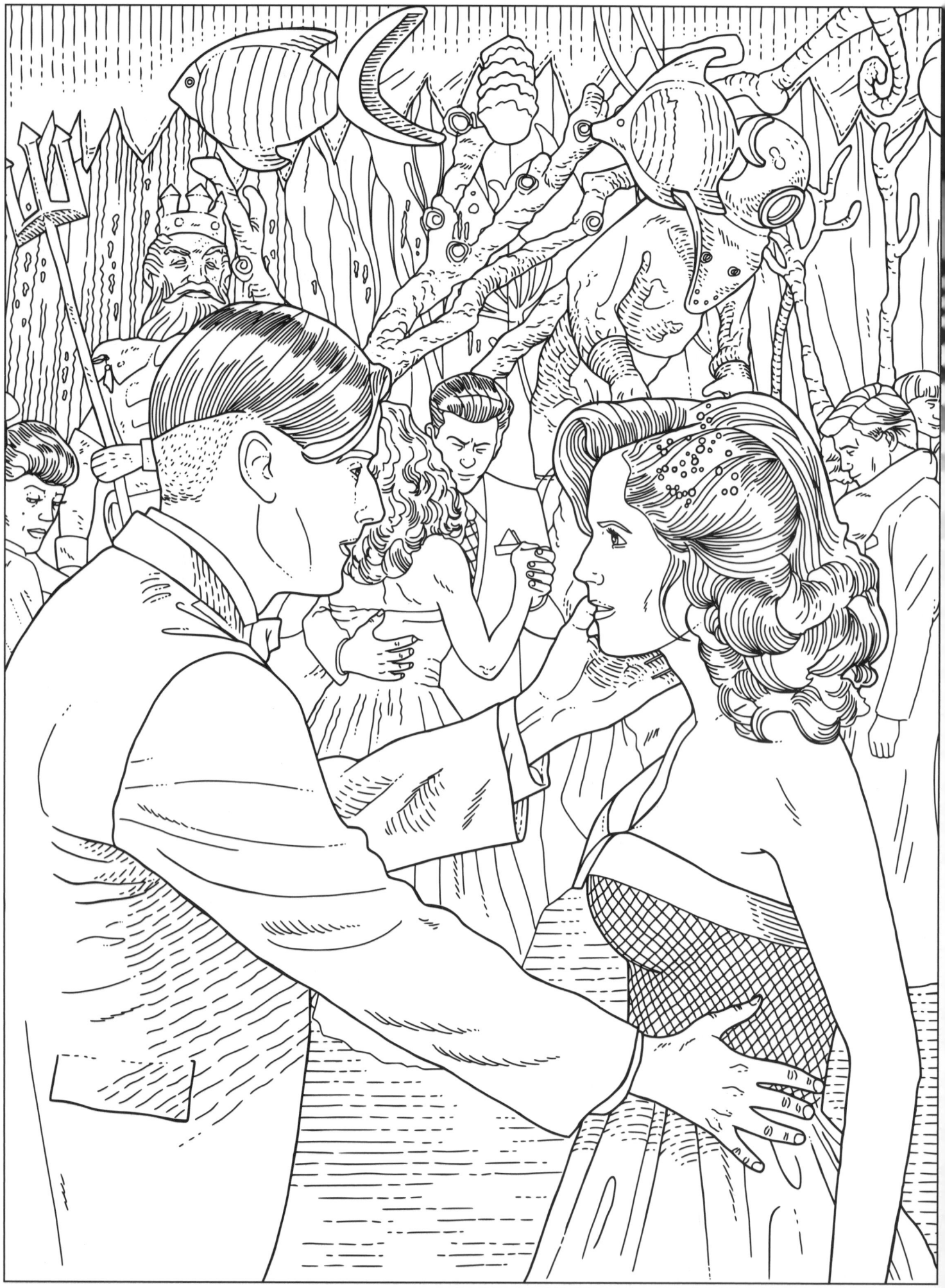

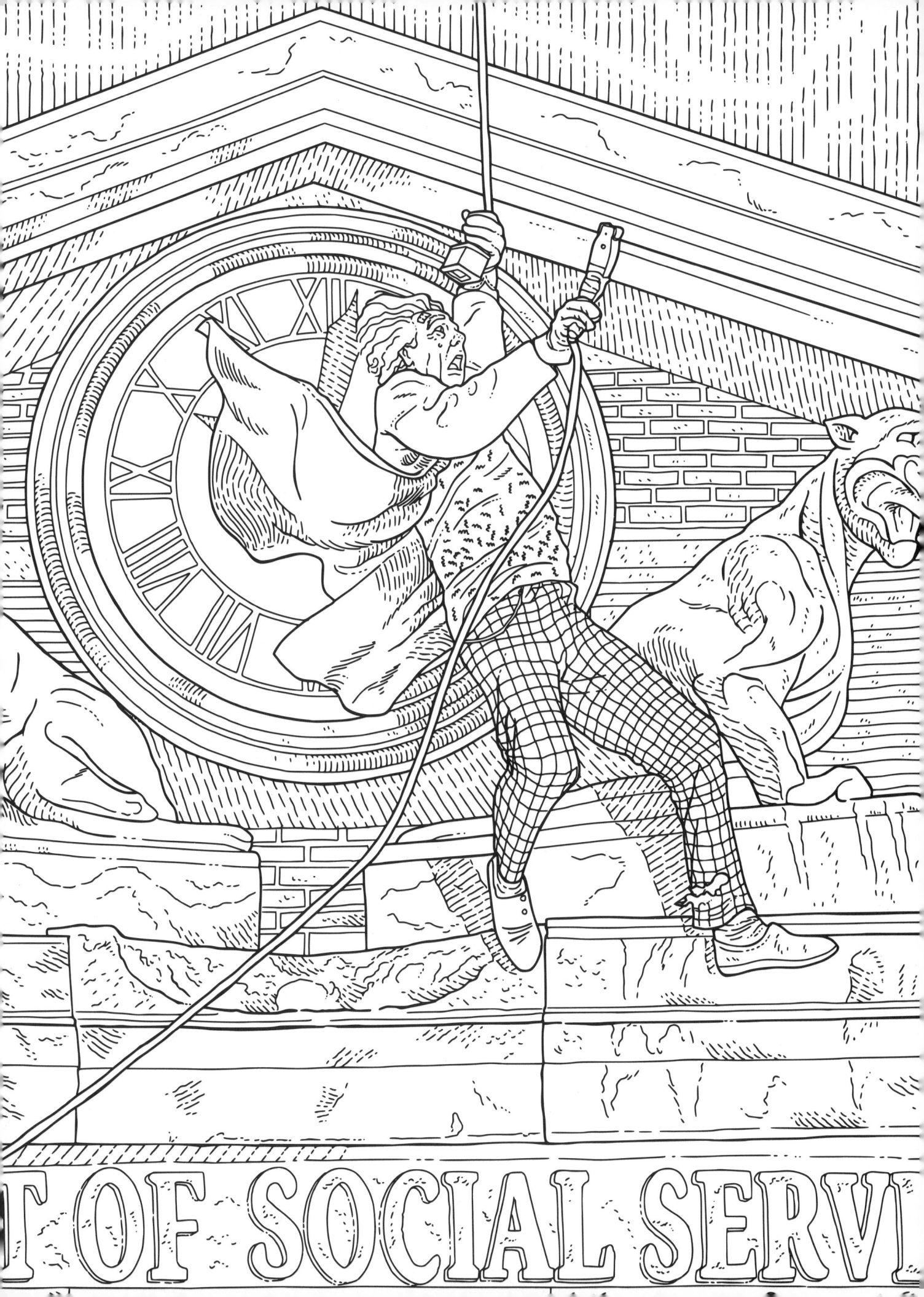
T OF SOCIAL SERVI

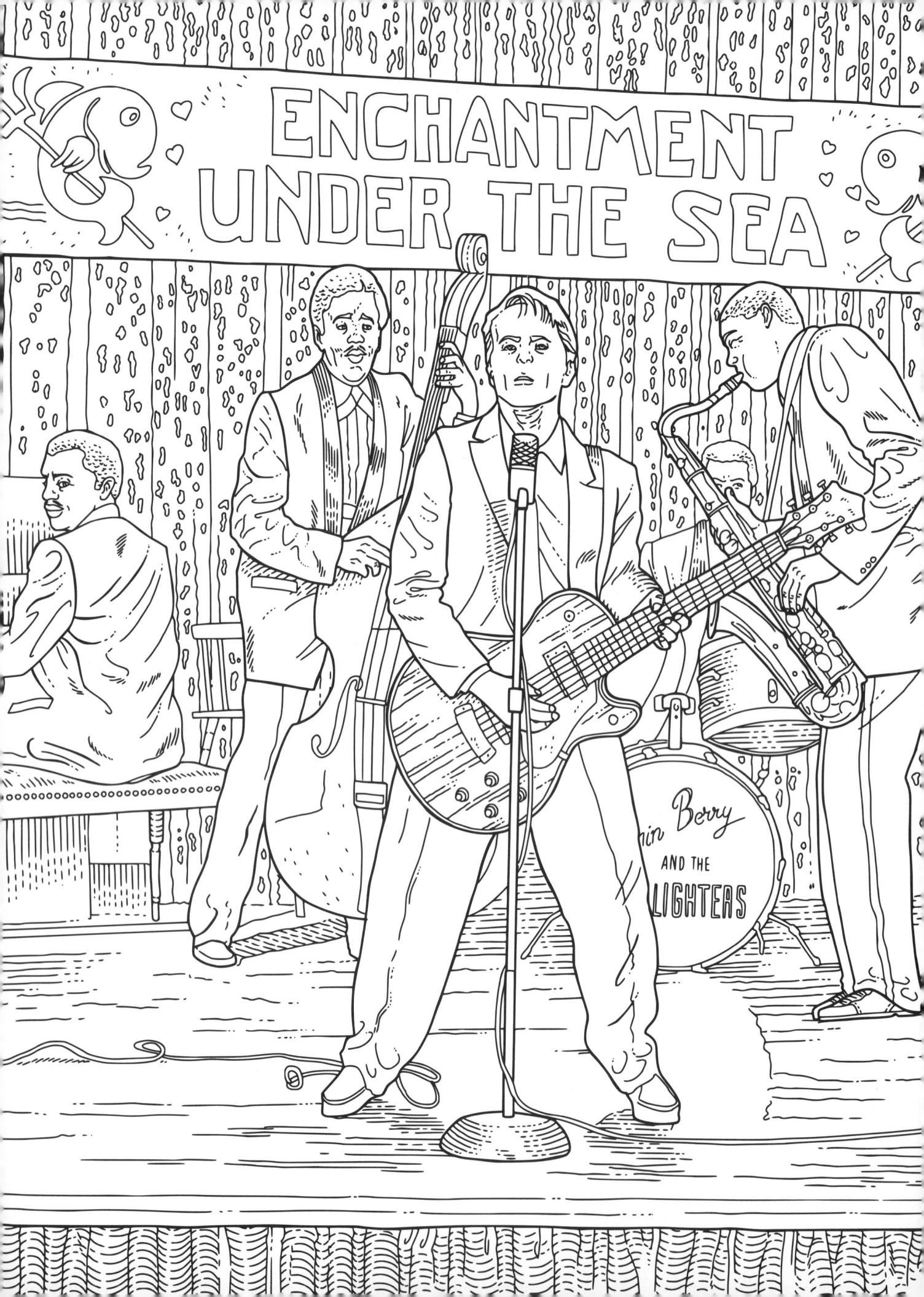
ENCHANTMENT
UNDER THE SEA
in Berry
AND THE
LIGHTERS

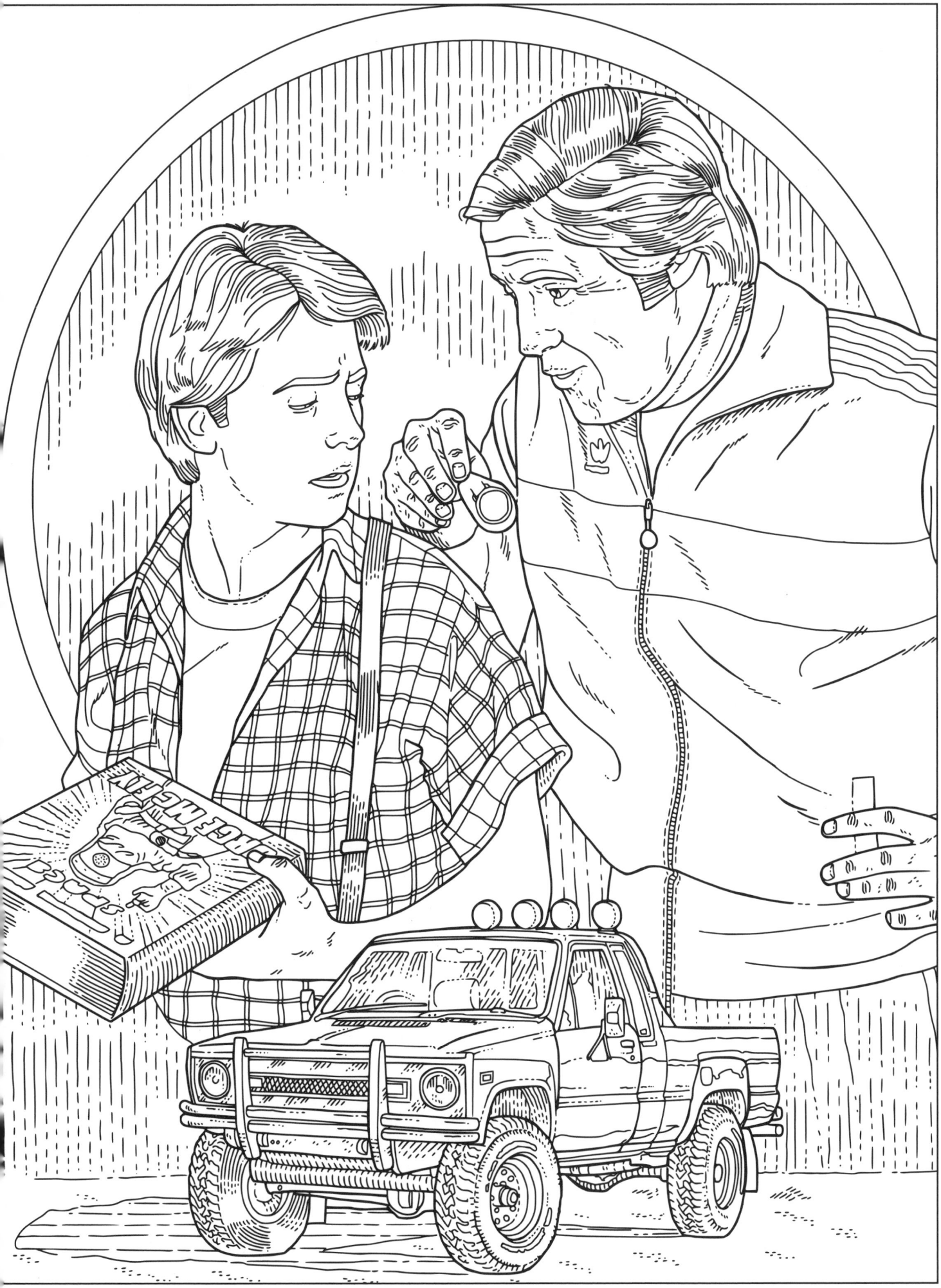

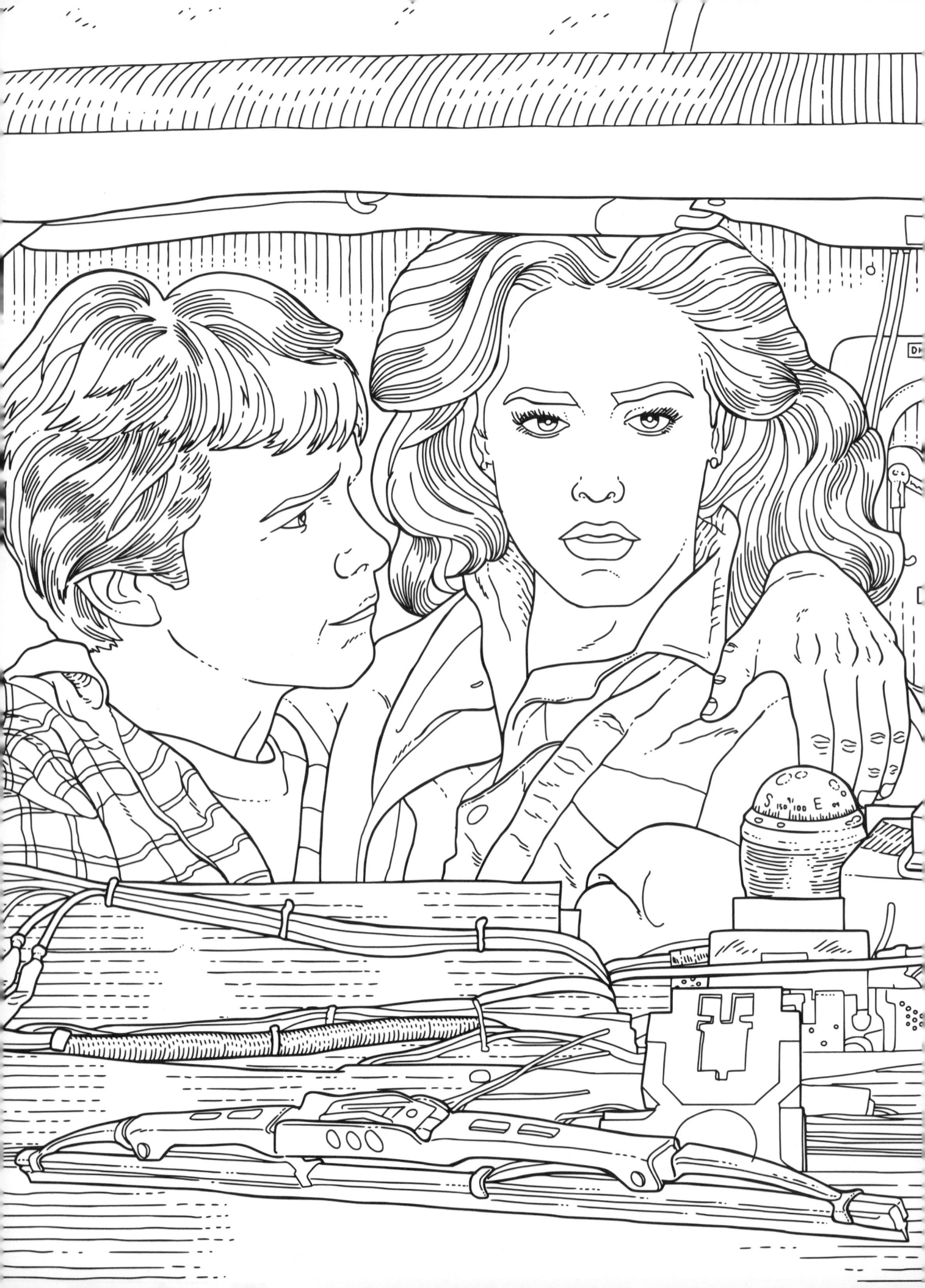
S 150 100 E

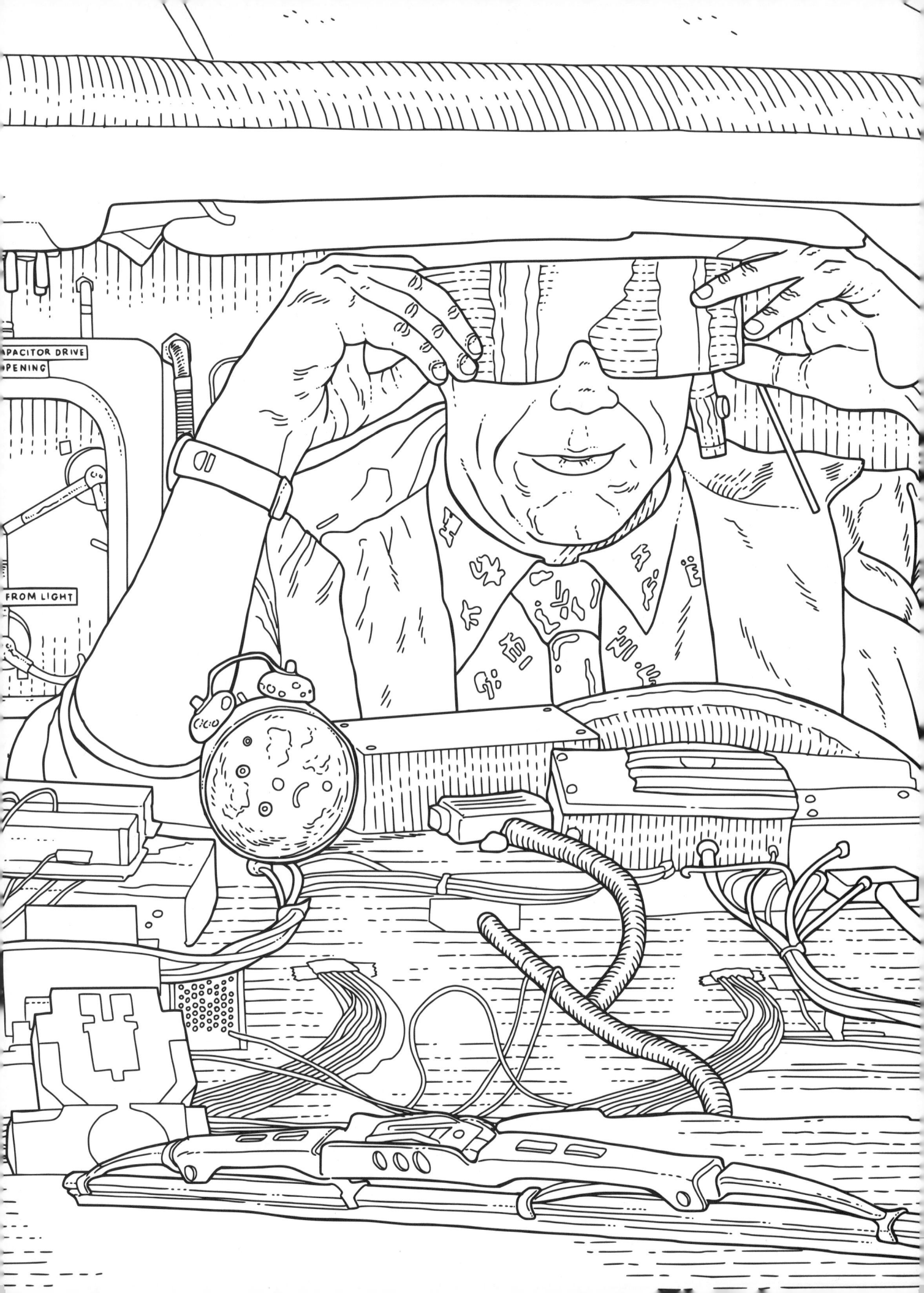
PACITOR DRIVE
PENING
FROM LIGHT

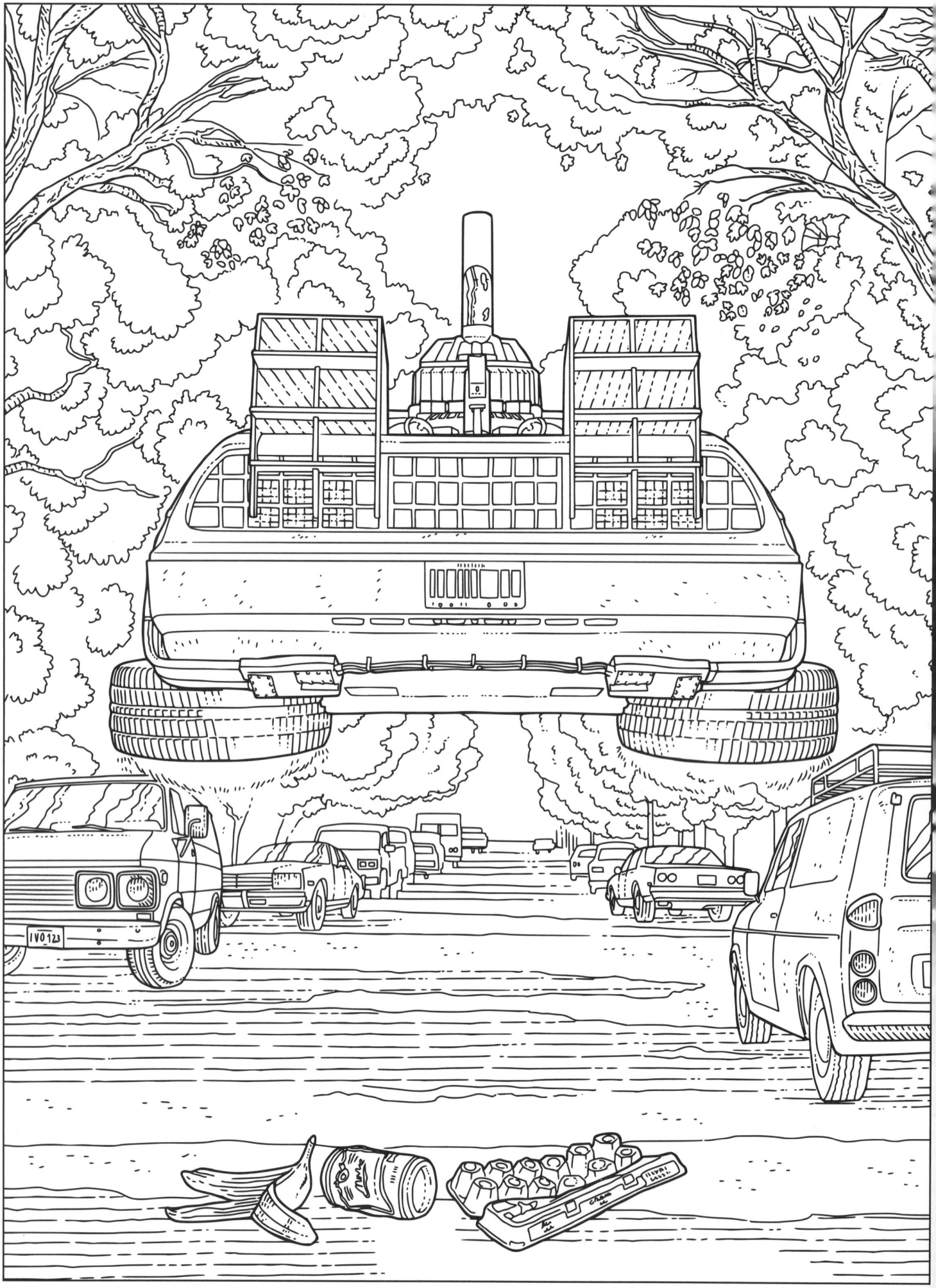

22A33
Re-Elect
MAYOR
WILSON
JR.
MAY
WILS
AUTION
CONE
TODAY
YOUTH JAILED

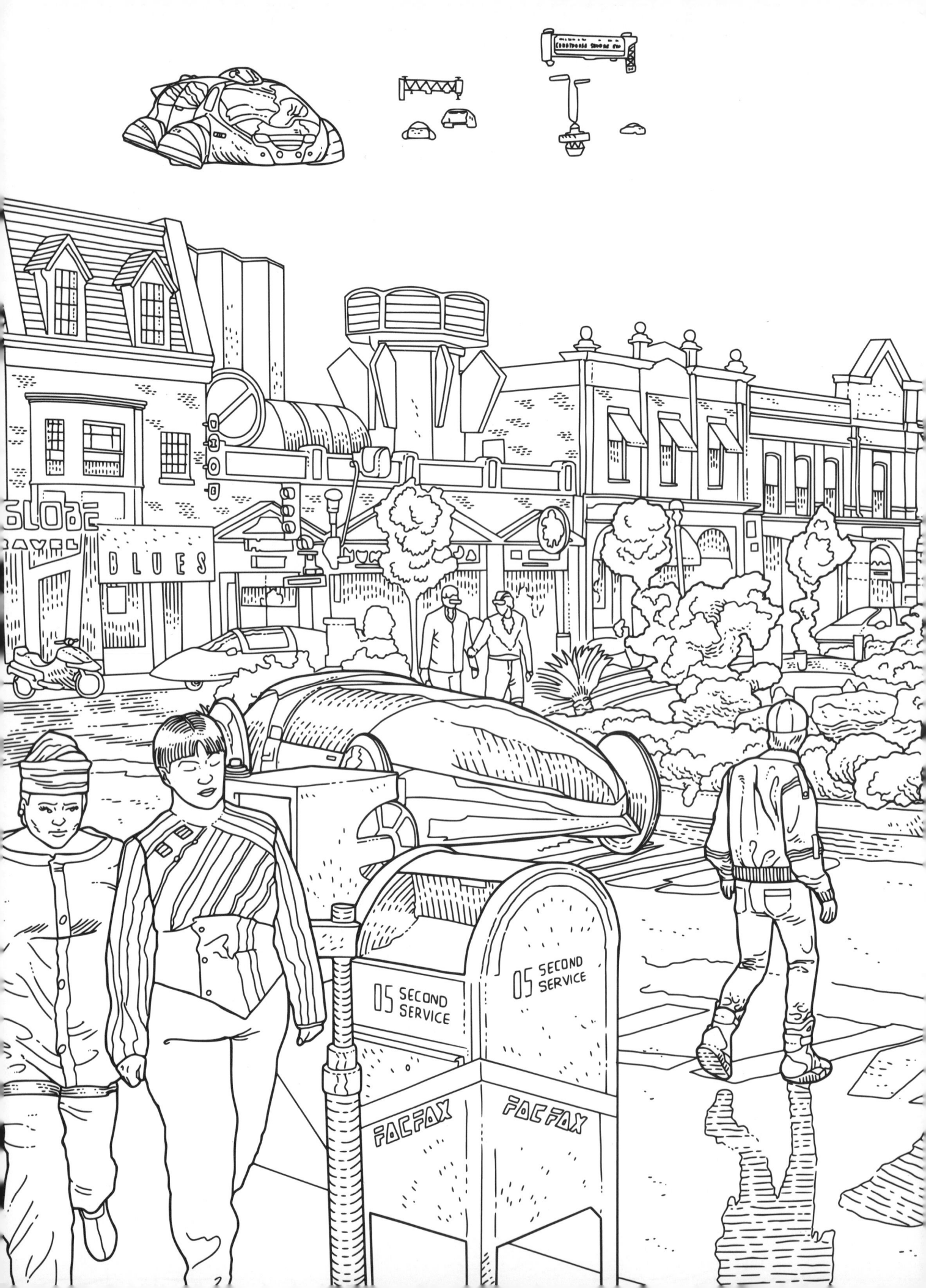
BLUES
05 SECOND SERVICE
05 SECOND SERVICE
FACFAX
FACFAX

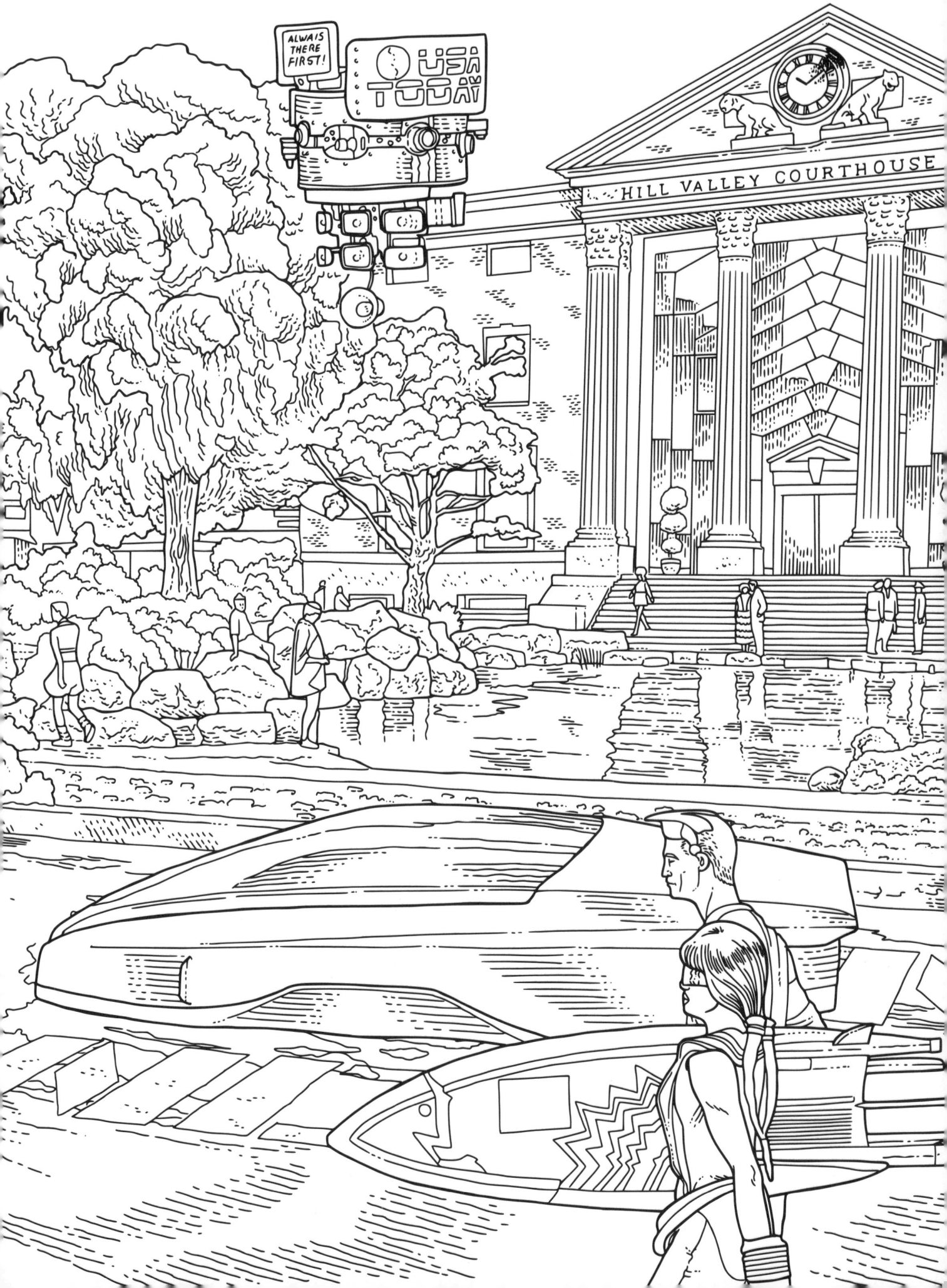
ALWAYS THERE FIRST!
USA TODAY
HILL VALLEY COURTHOUSE

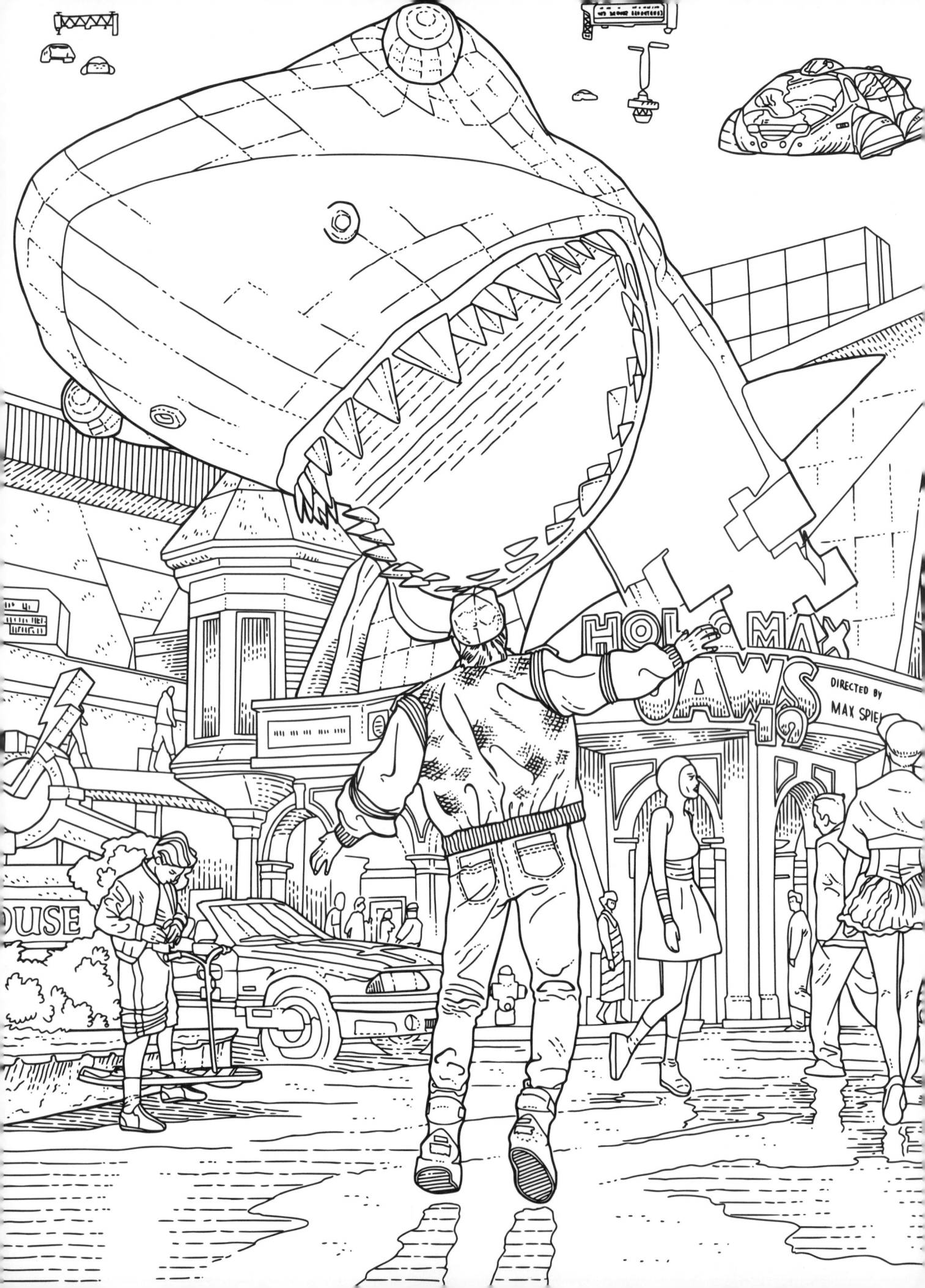
HOL MAX
JAWS
DIRECTED BY
MAX SPIE
OUSE

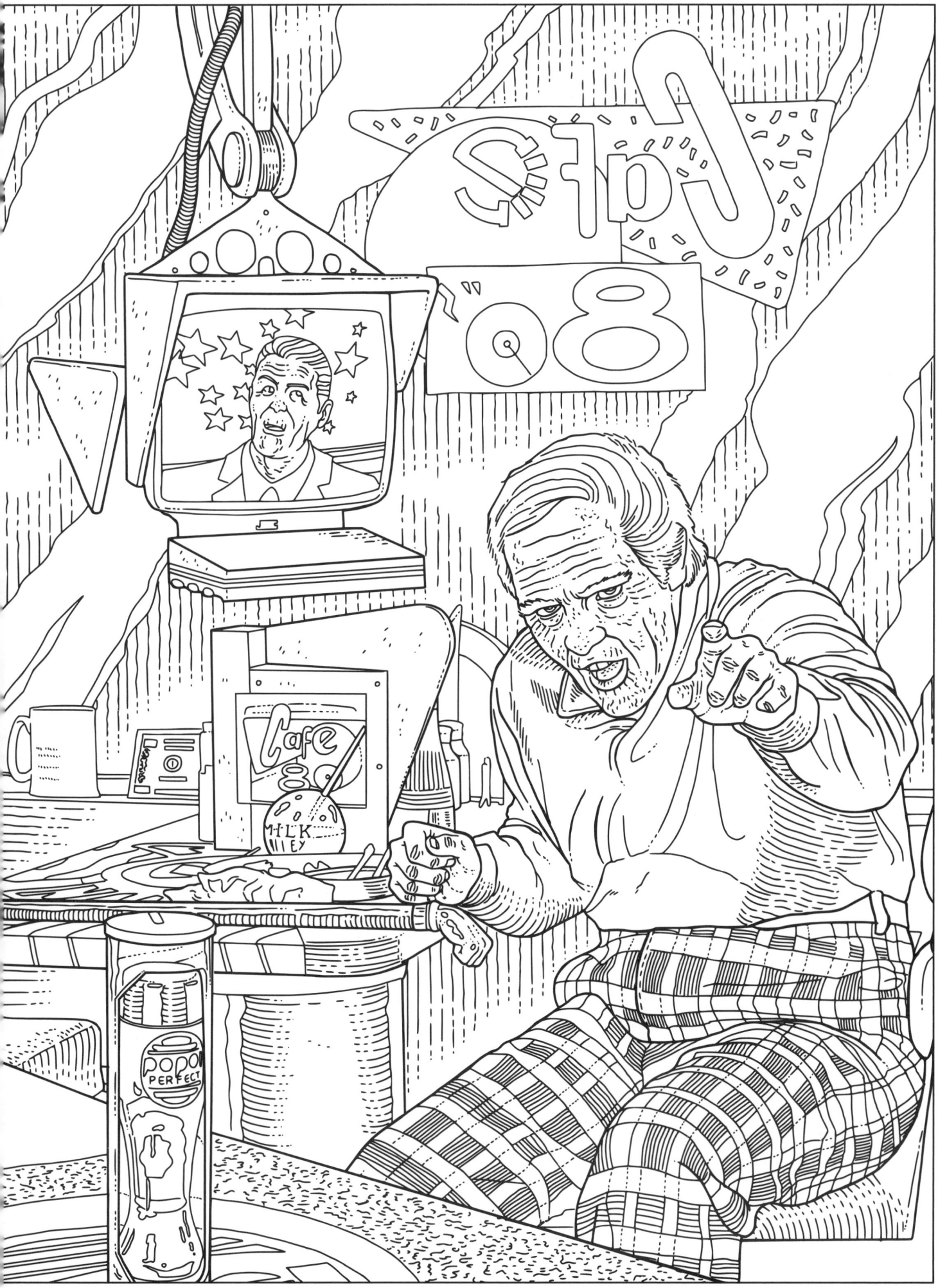
Cafe
MILK
PERFECT

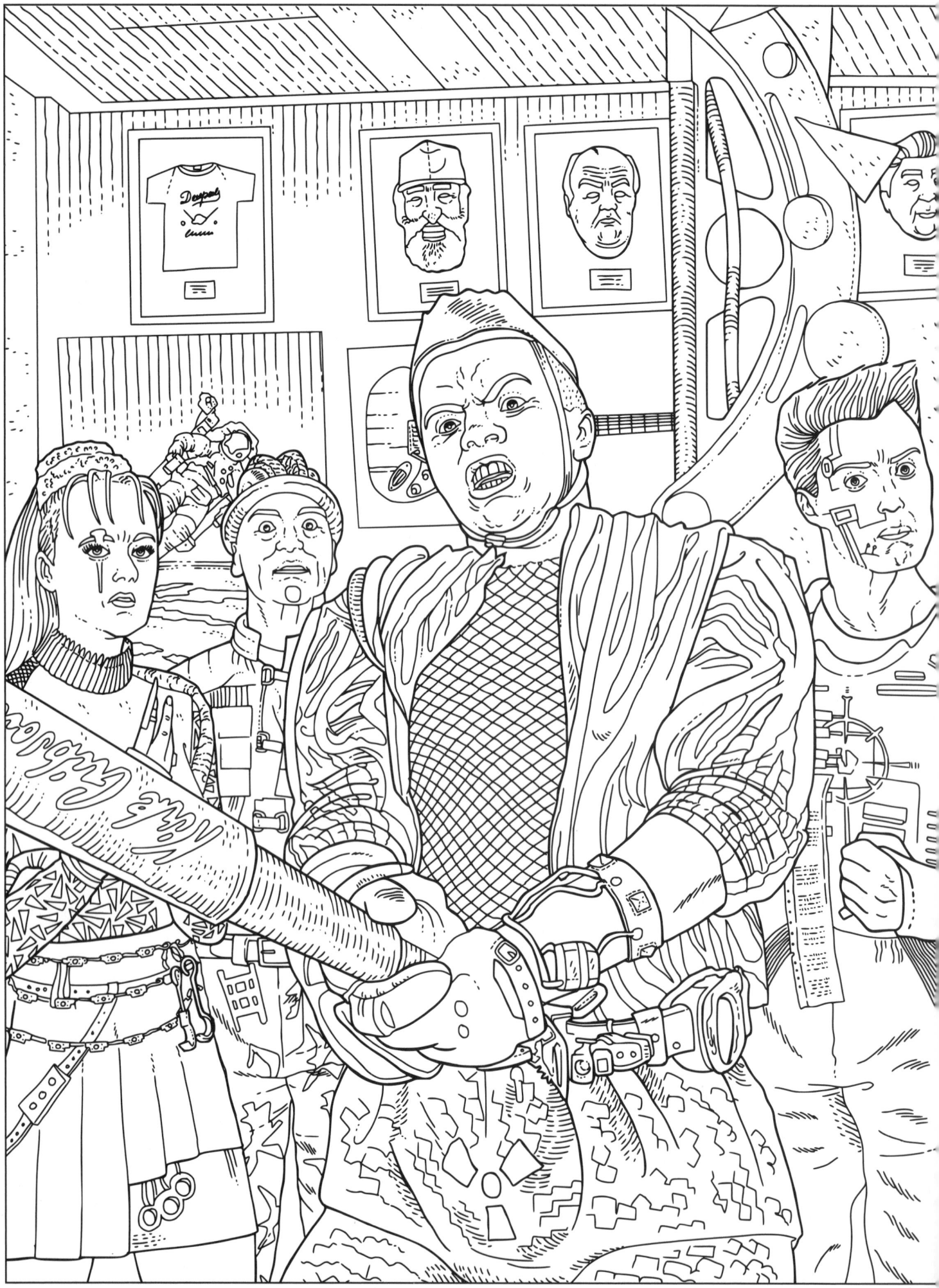

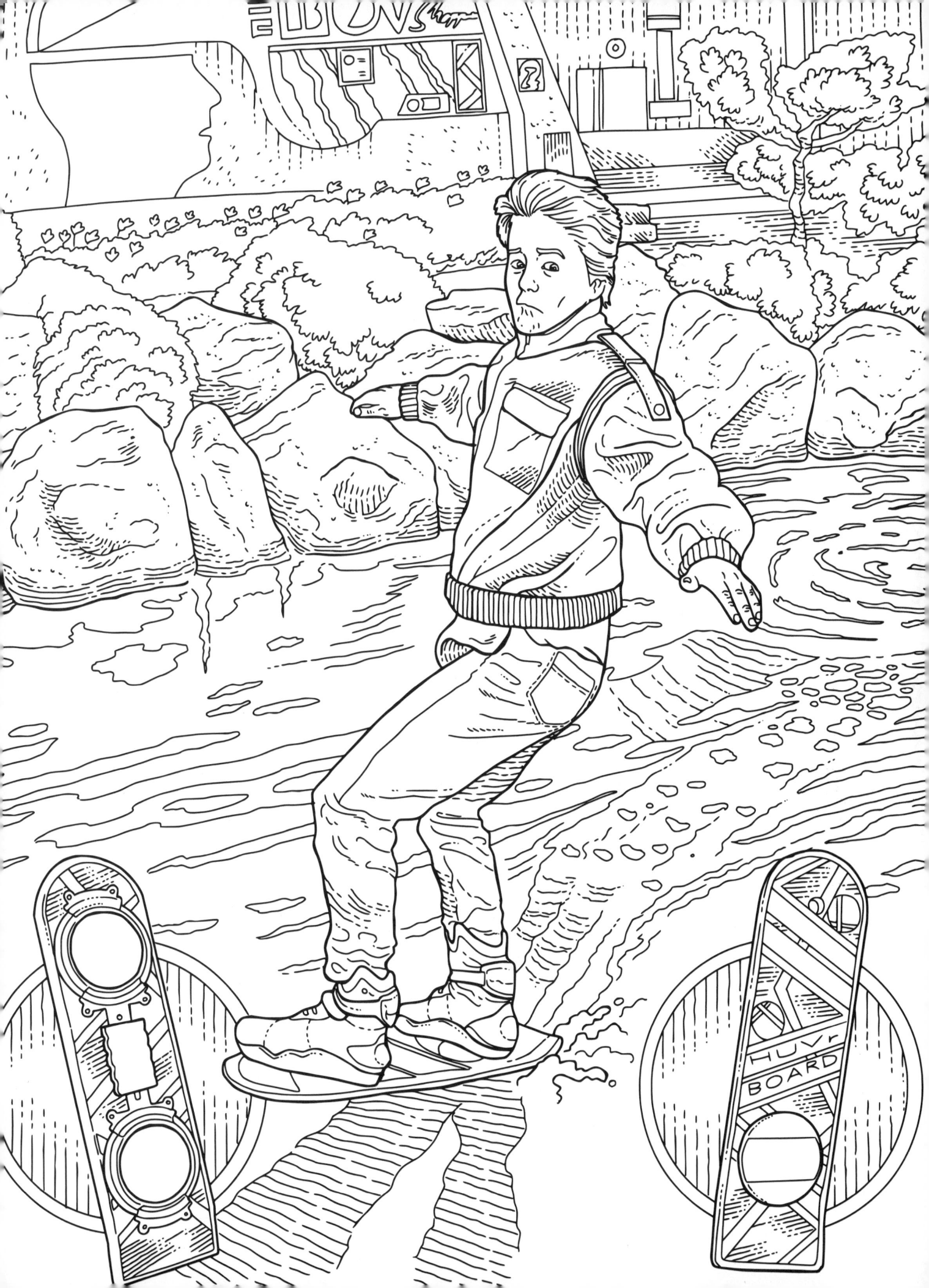
HUVr
BOARD

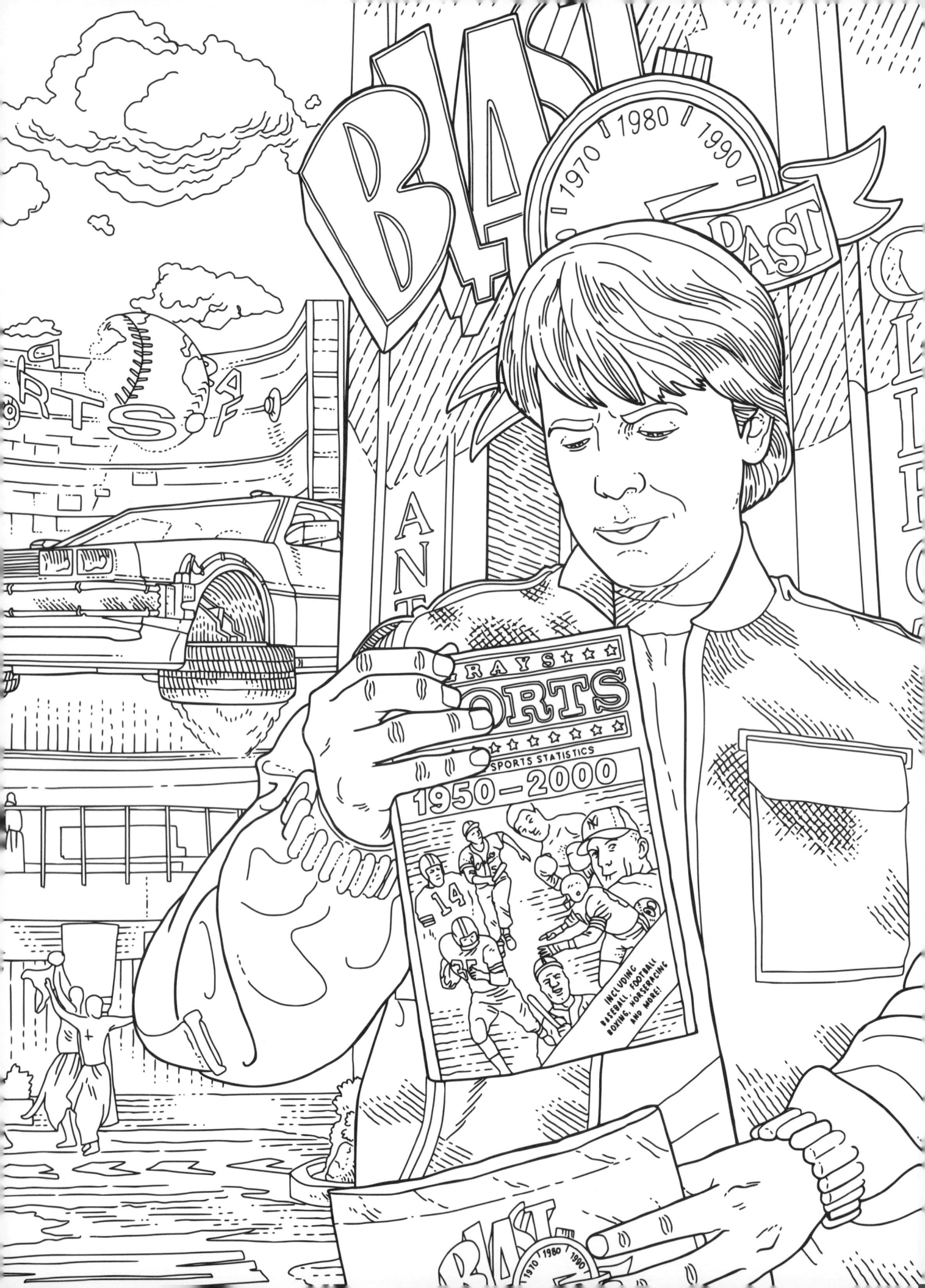
1970 1980 1990
RAYS
SPORTS
SPORTS STATISTICS
1950–2000
INCLUDING BASEBALL, FOOTBALL BOXING, HORSERACING AND MORE!

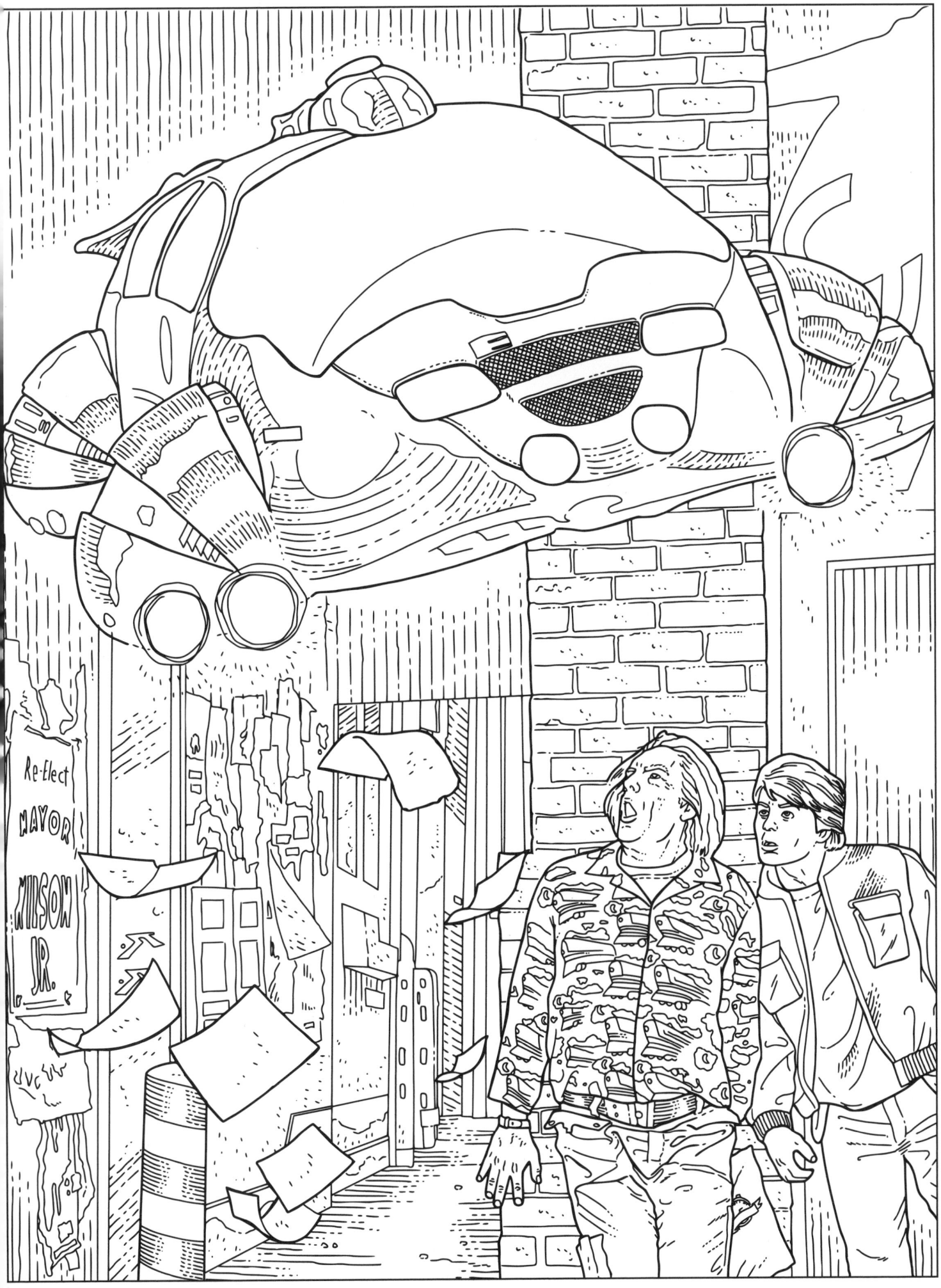
Re-Elect
MAYOR
MIDSON
JR.

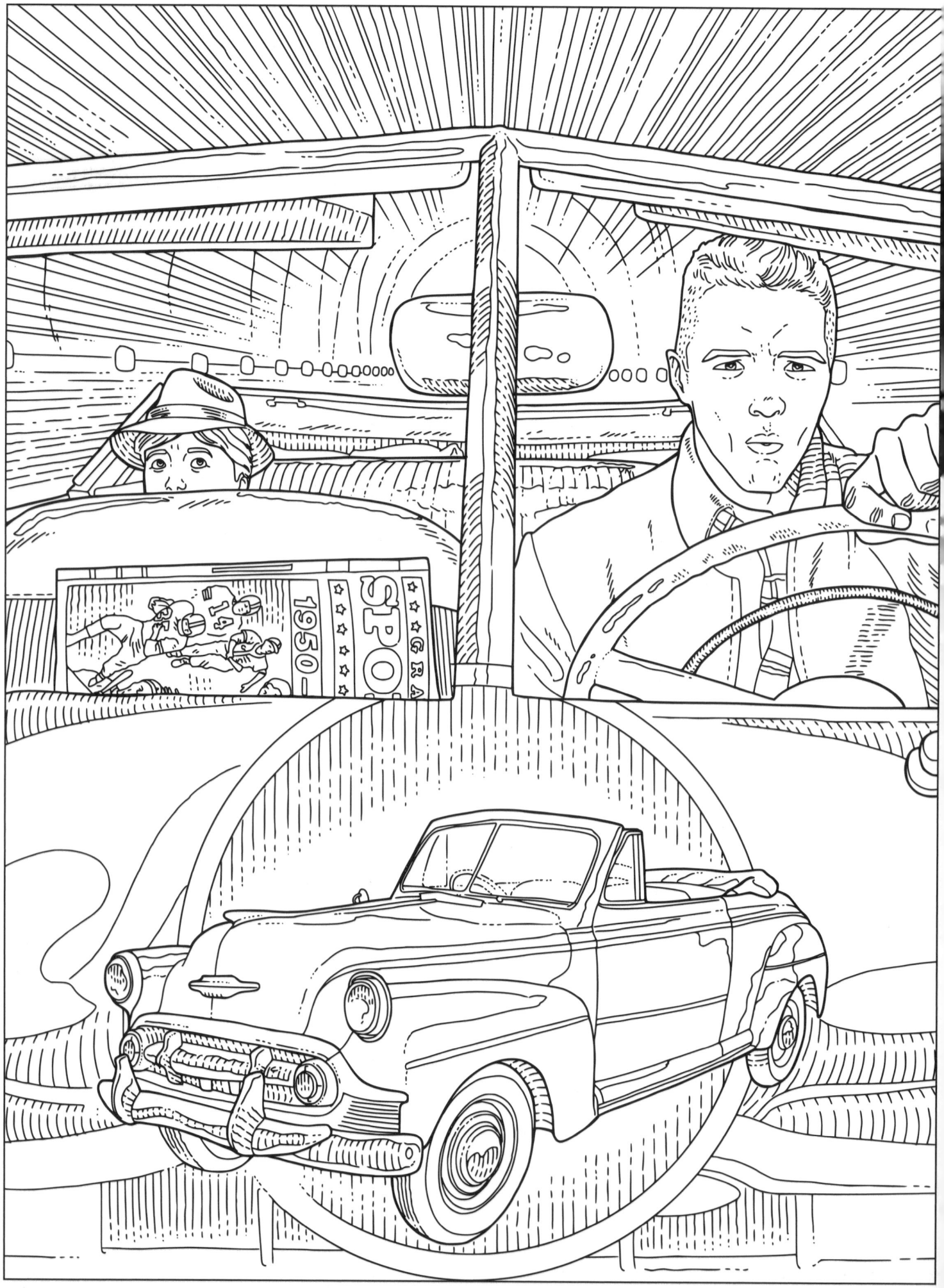
SPO
1950

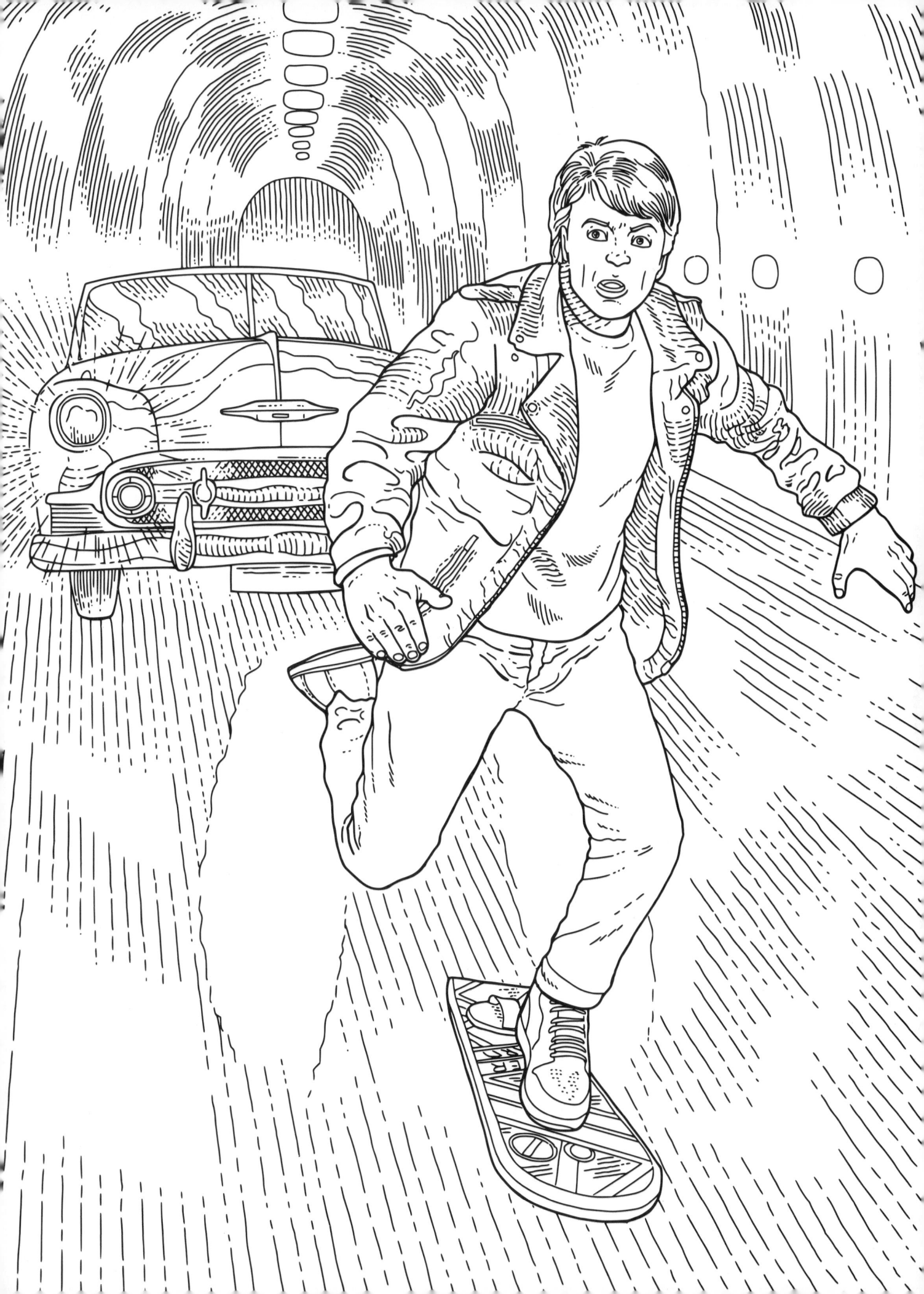

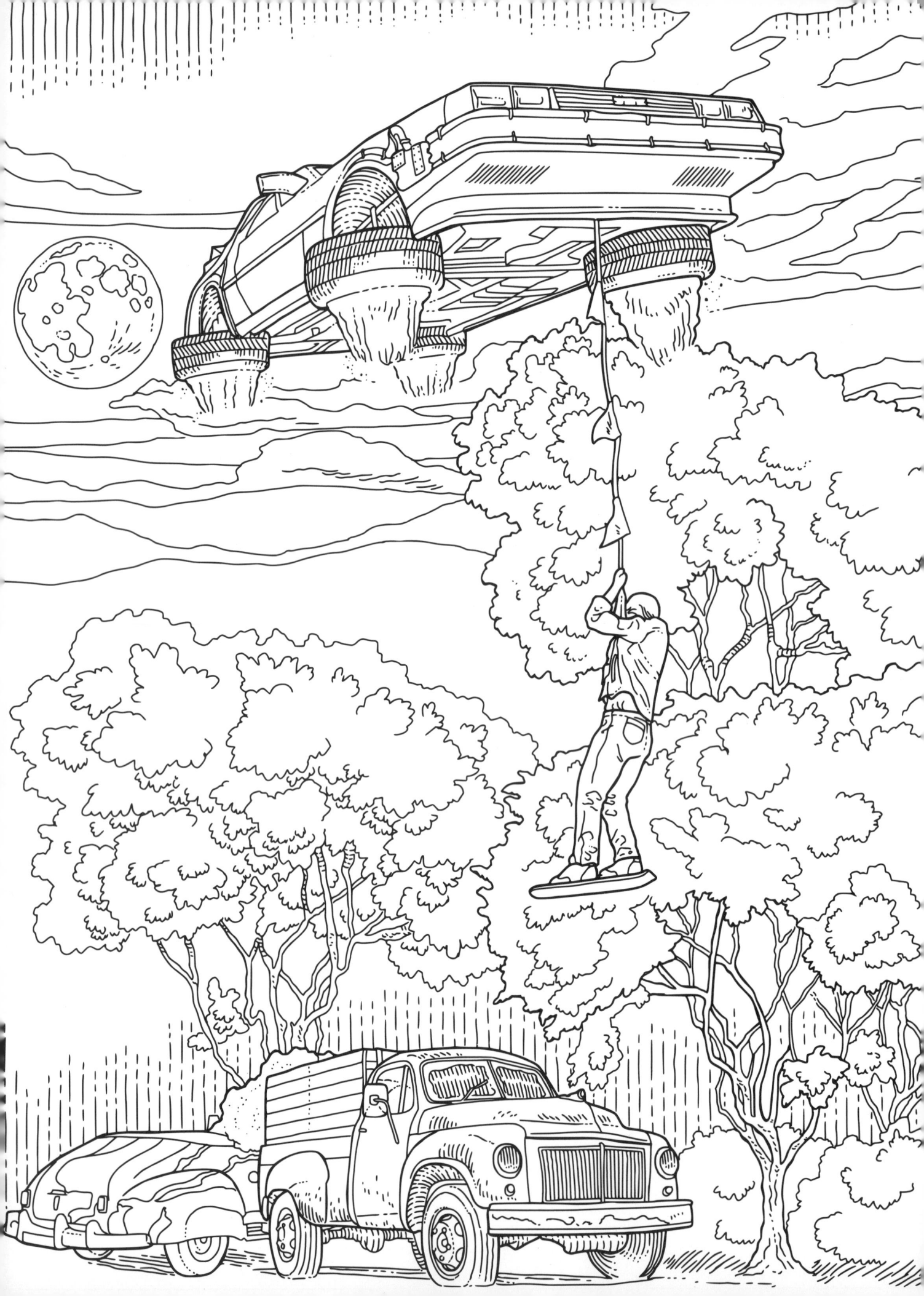

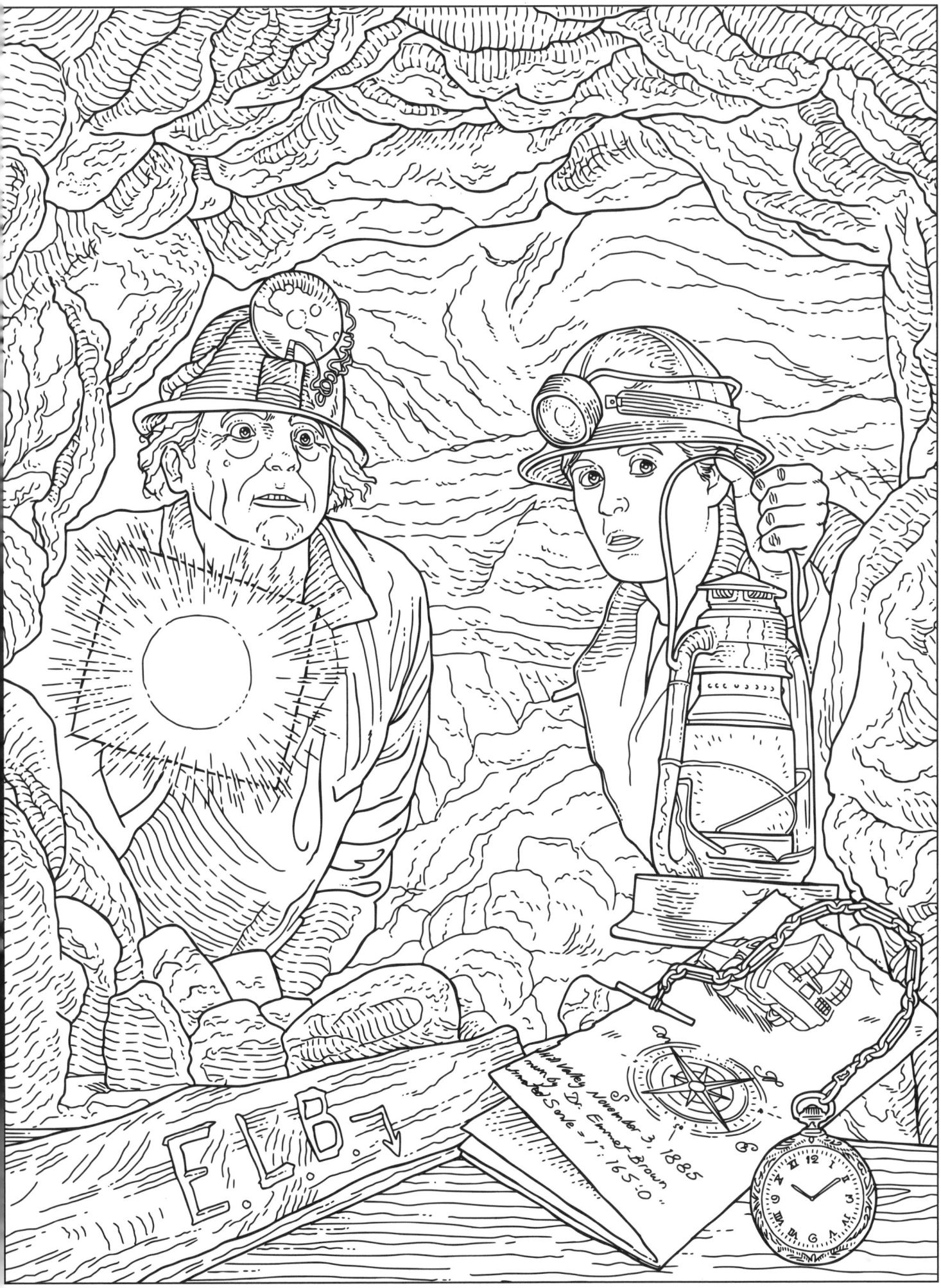
E.L.B.
November 3, 1885
Emmet Brown

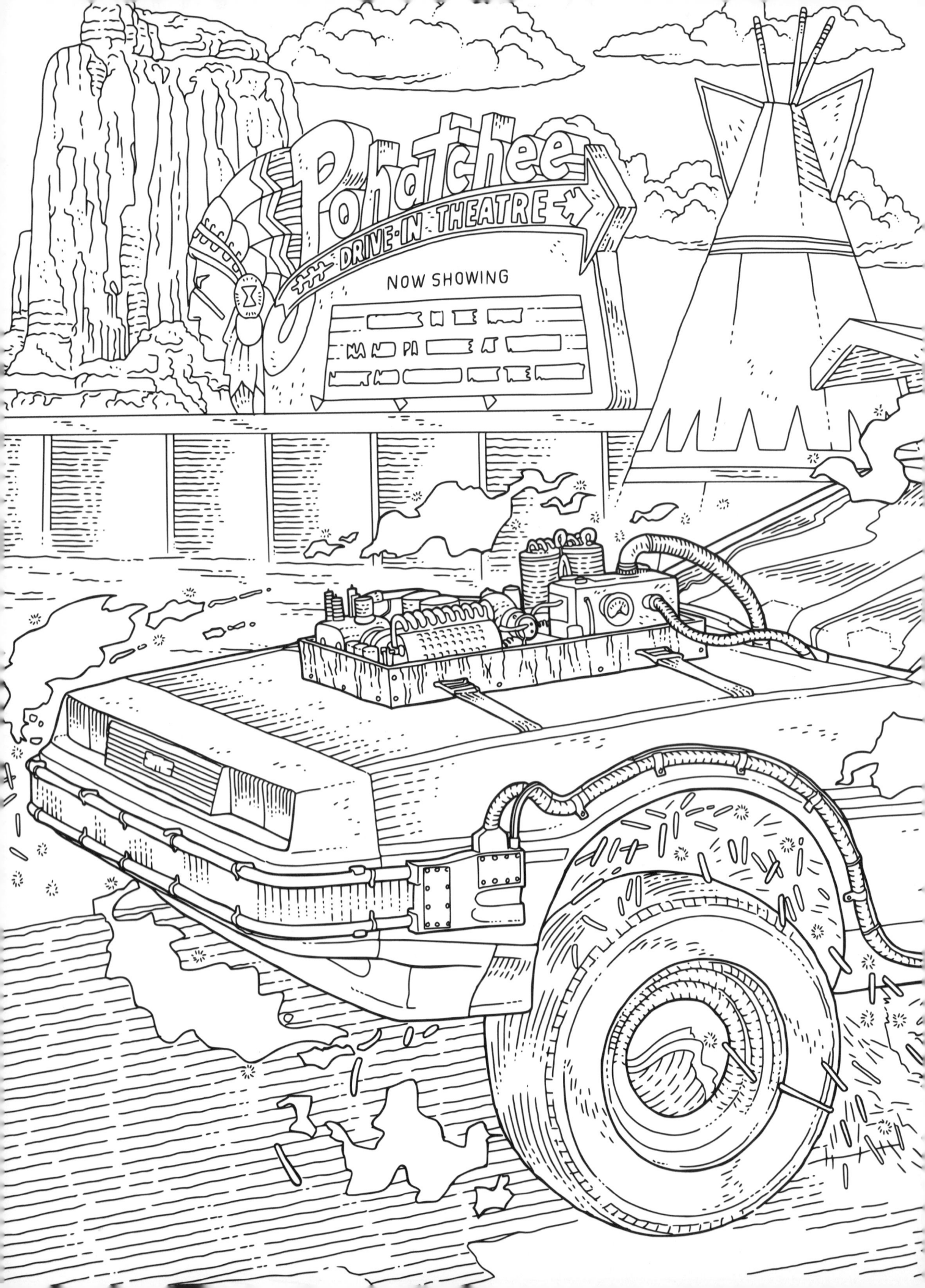
Pohatchee
DRIVE-IN THEATRE
NOW SHOWING
PA

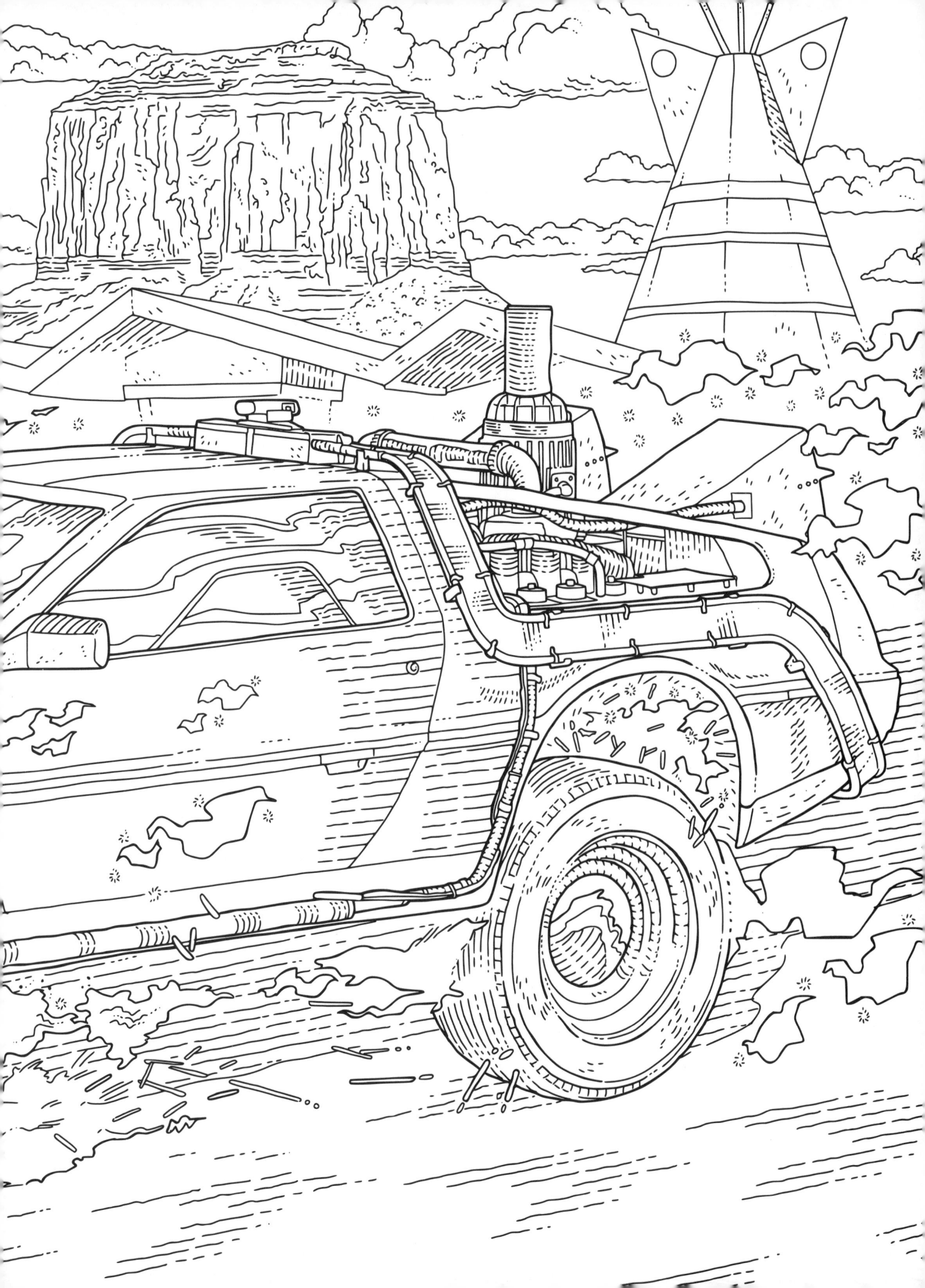

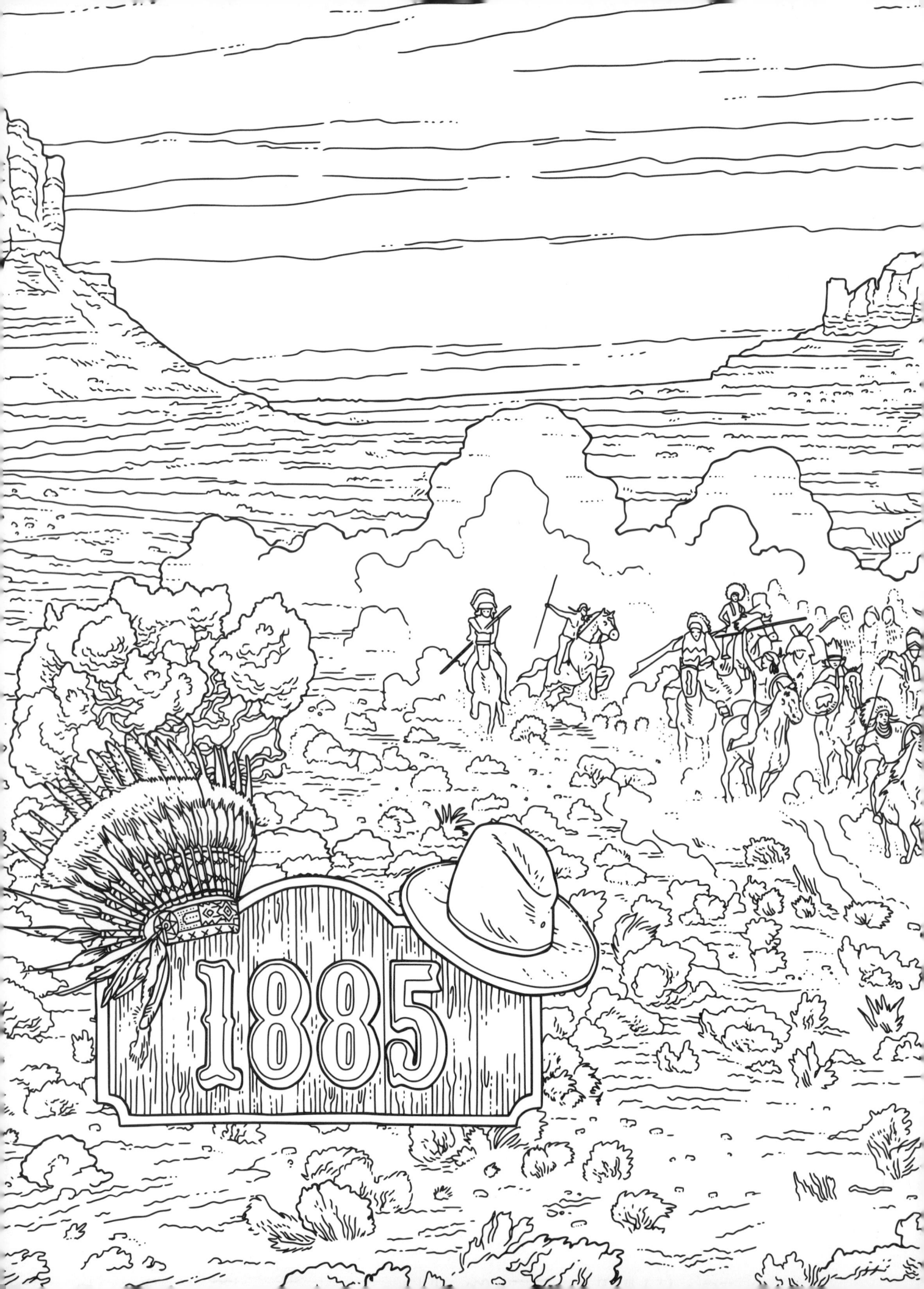
1885

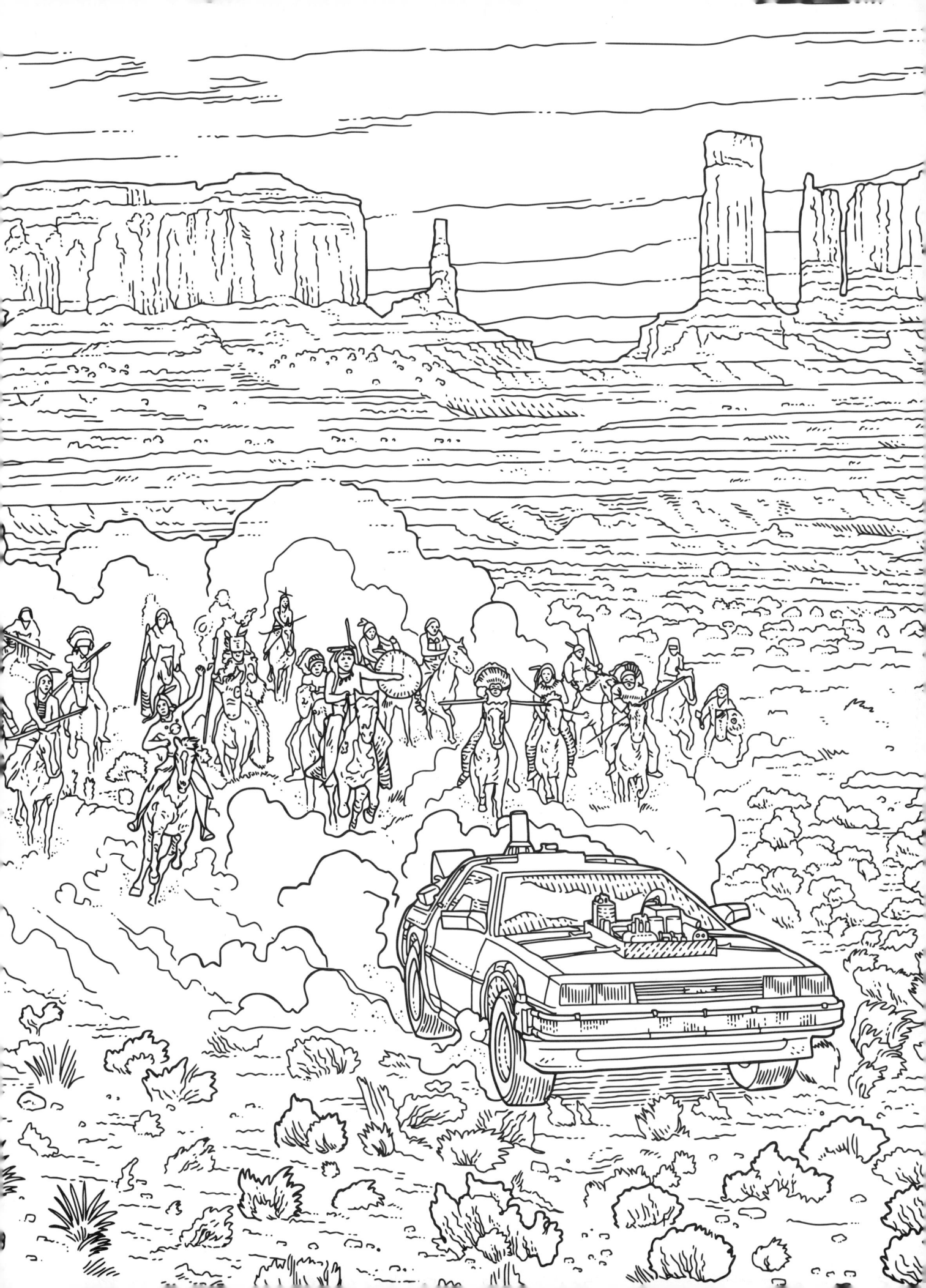

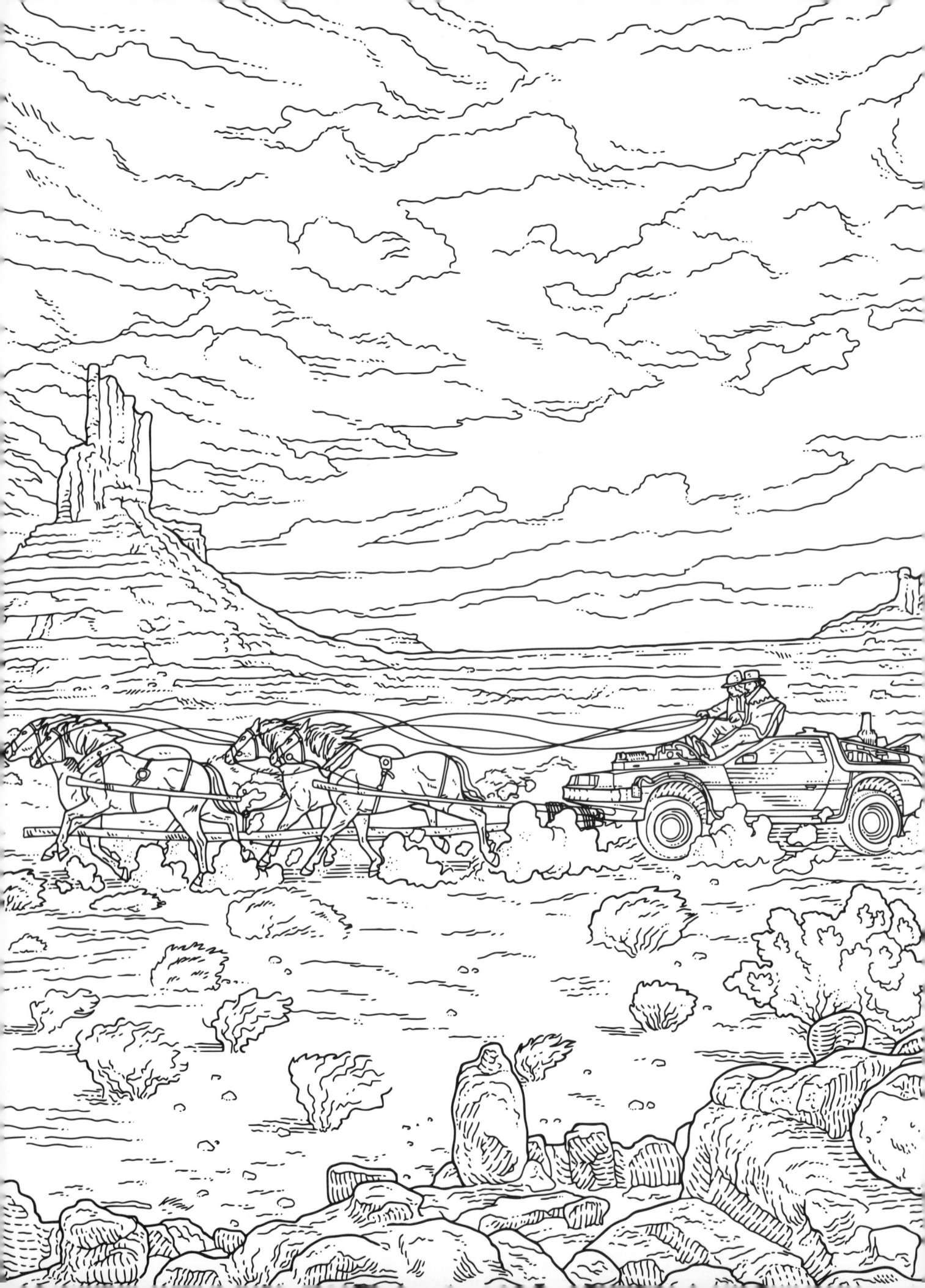

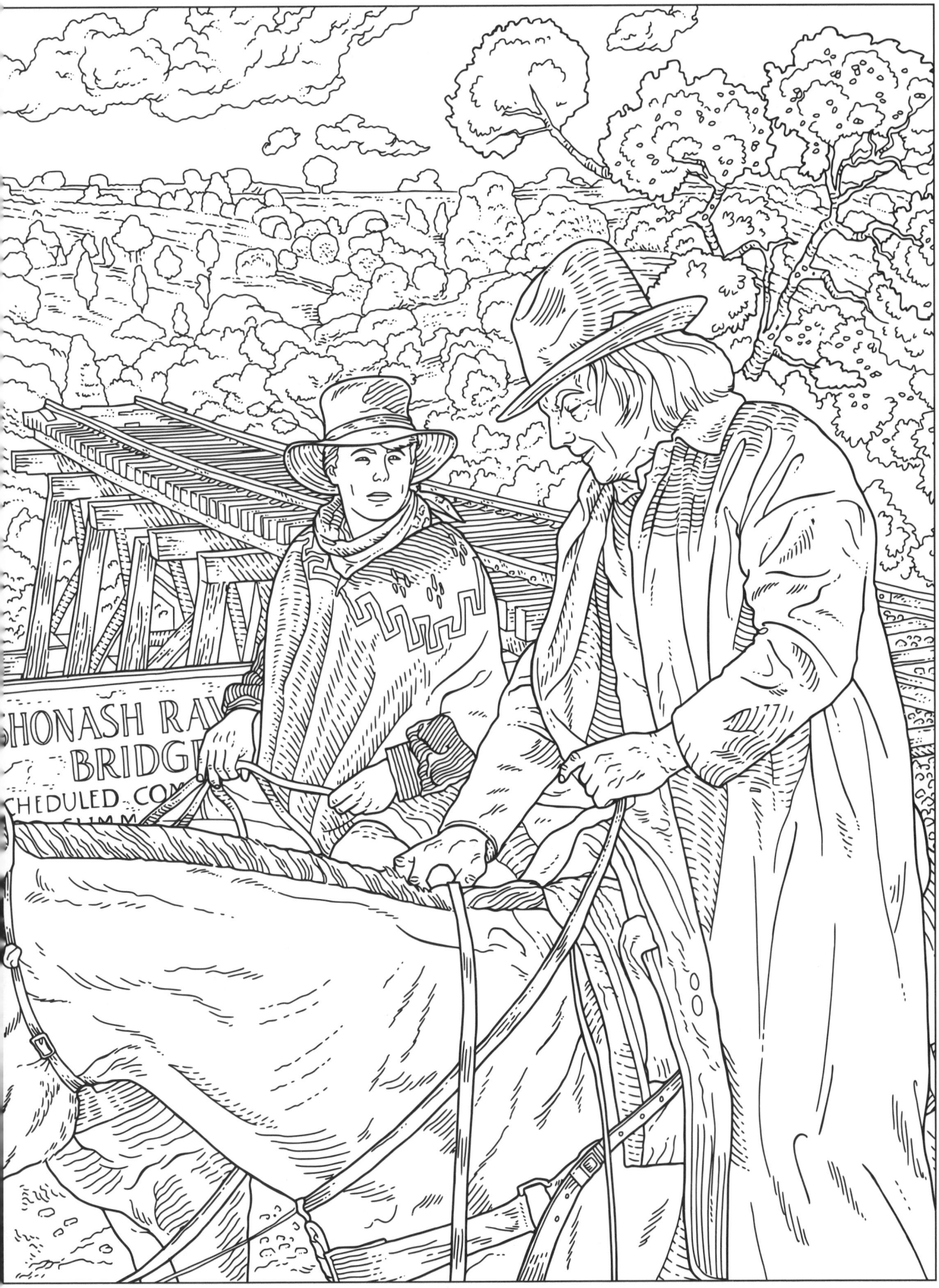
HONASH RA
BRIDGE
CHEDULED CON

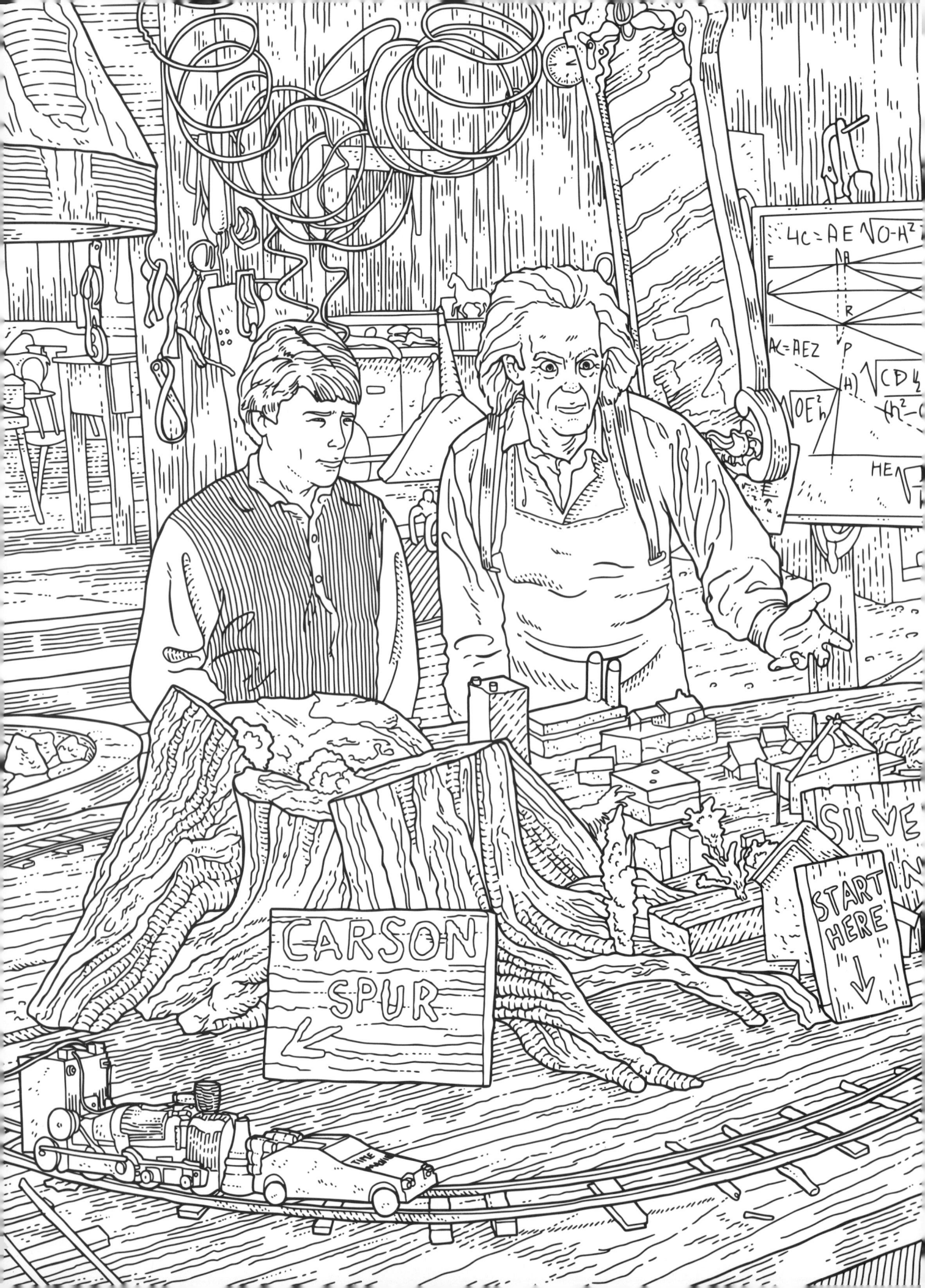
CARSON
SPUR
START
HERE
TIME

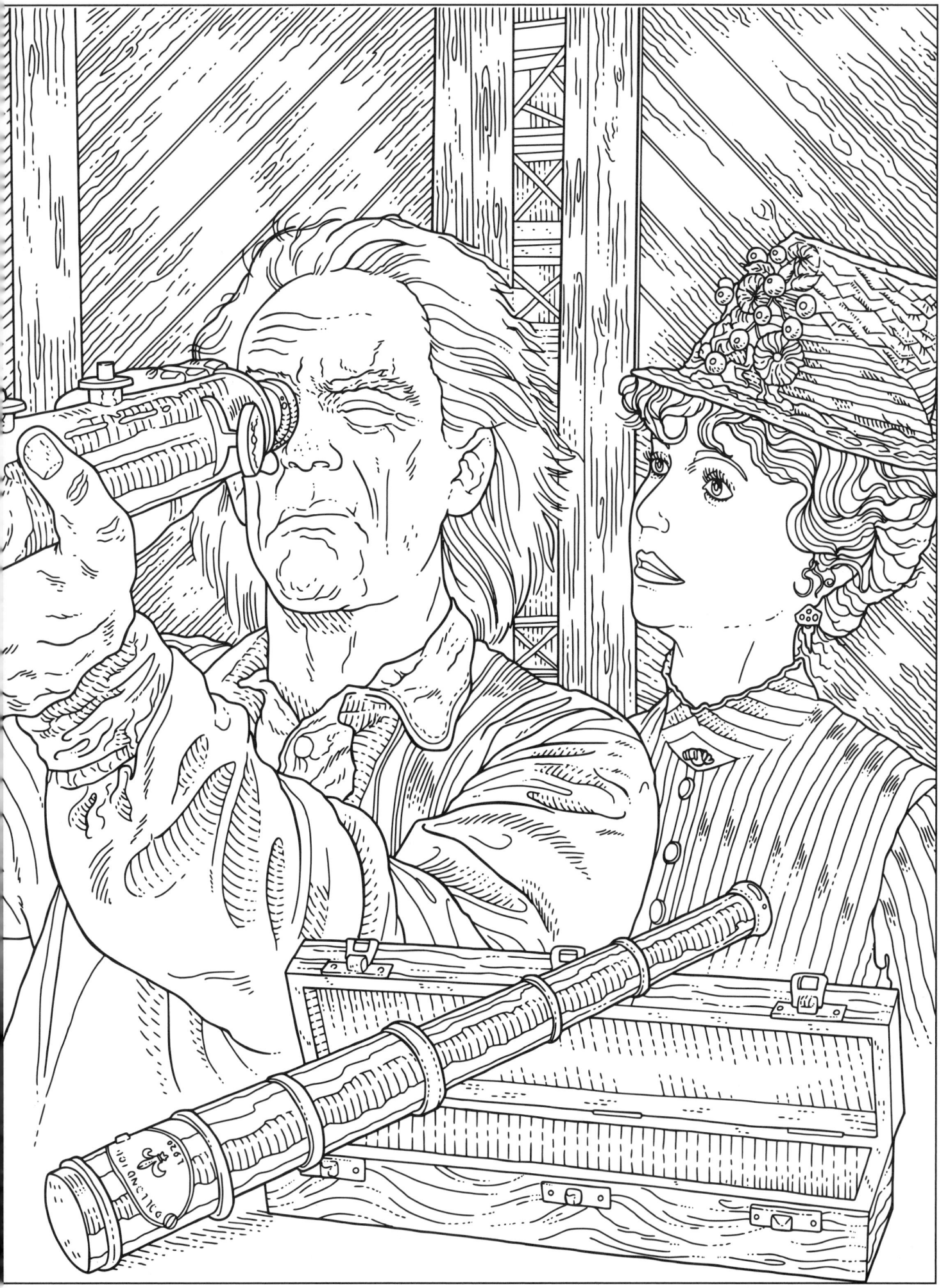

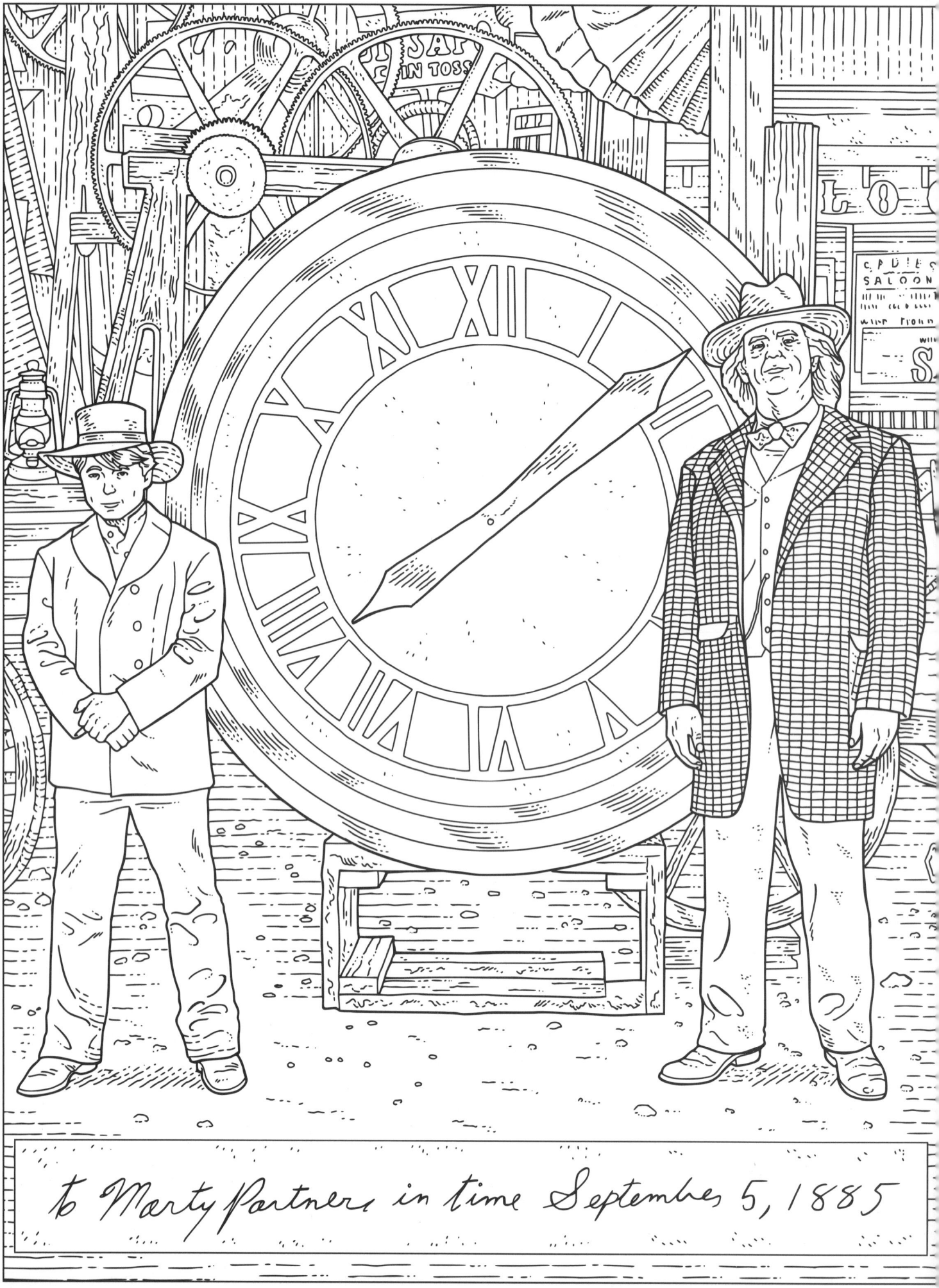
SAL
IN TOSS
SALOON
to Marty Partner in time September 5, 1885

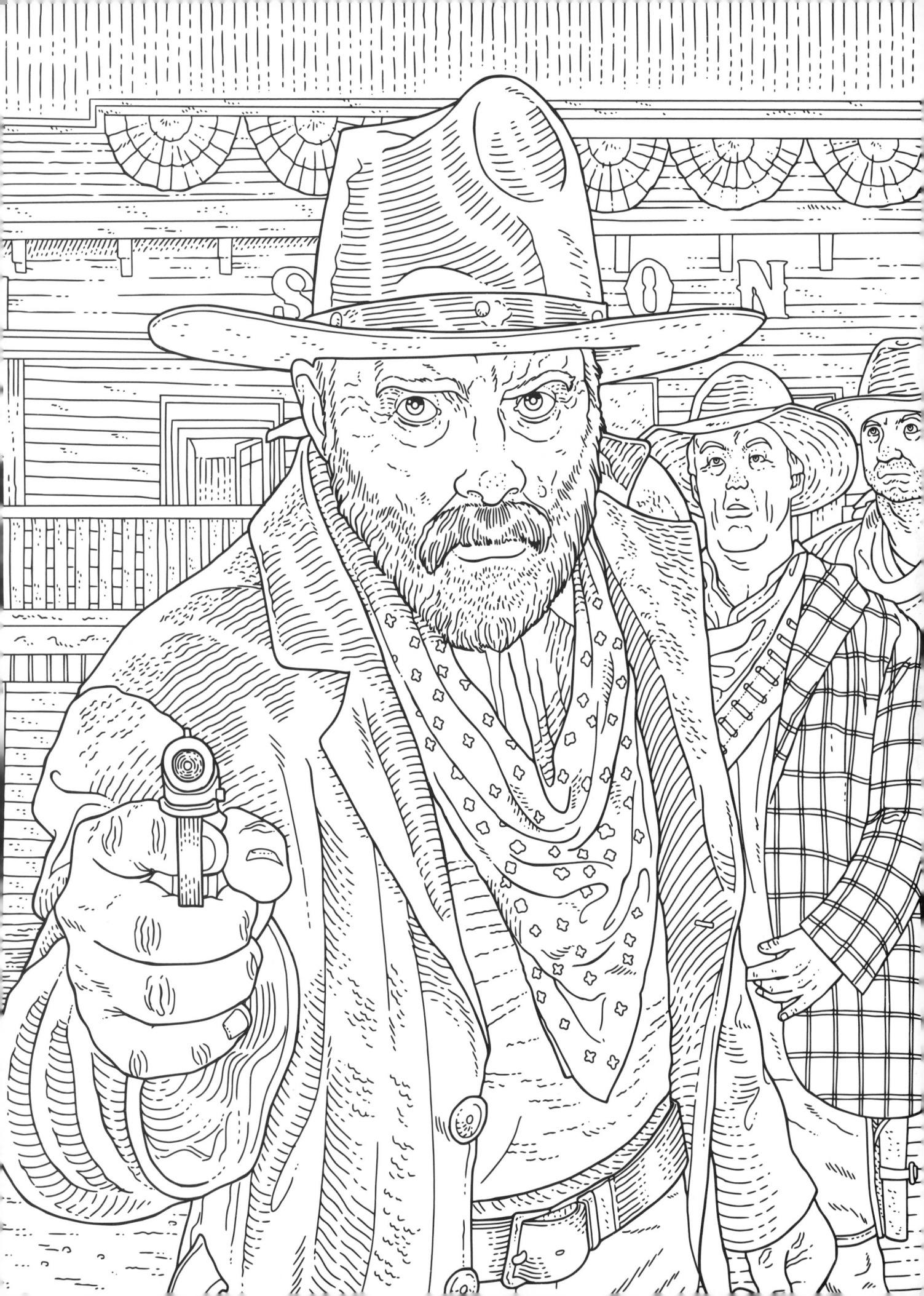
SALOON

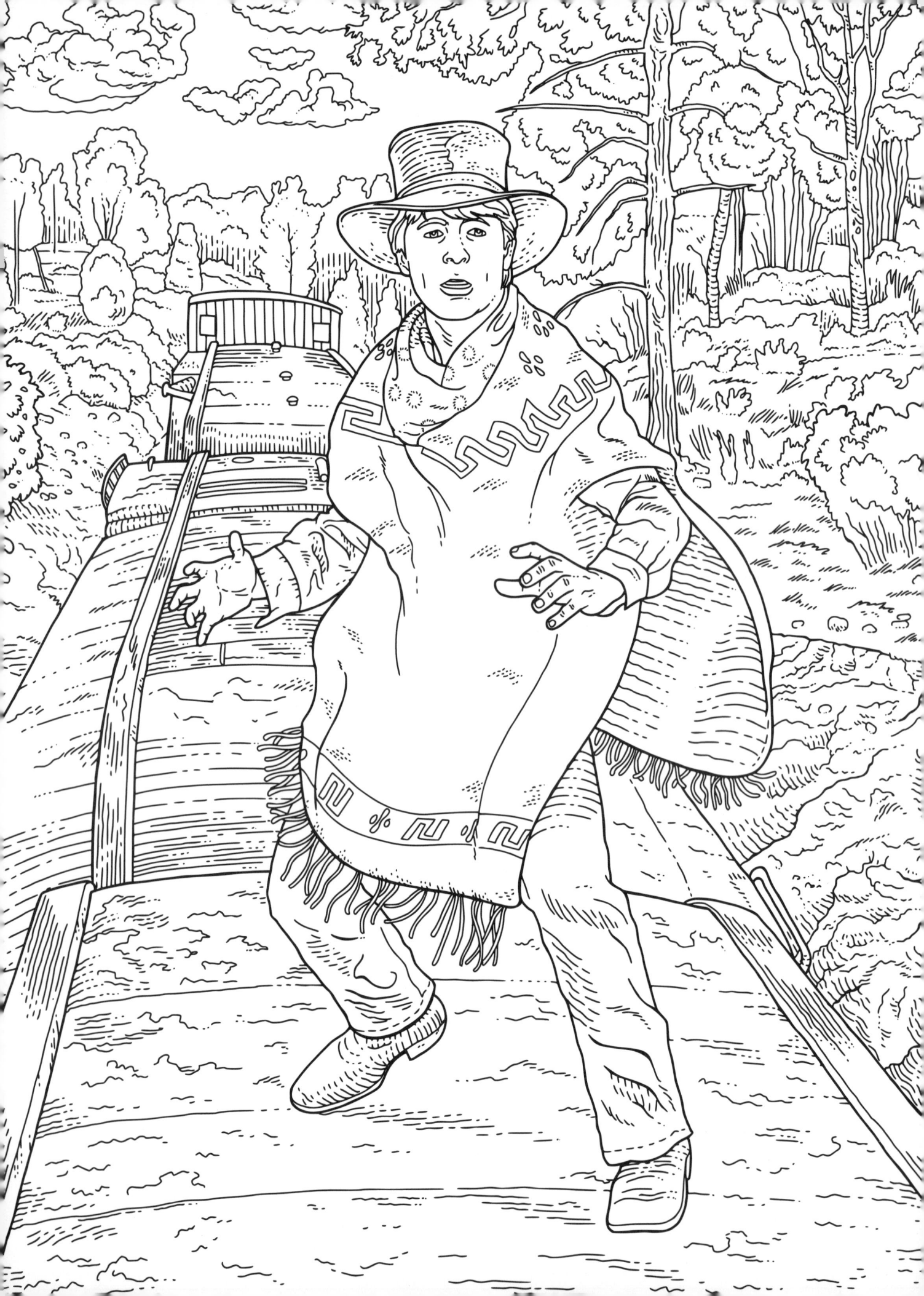

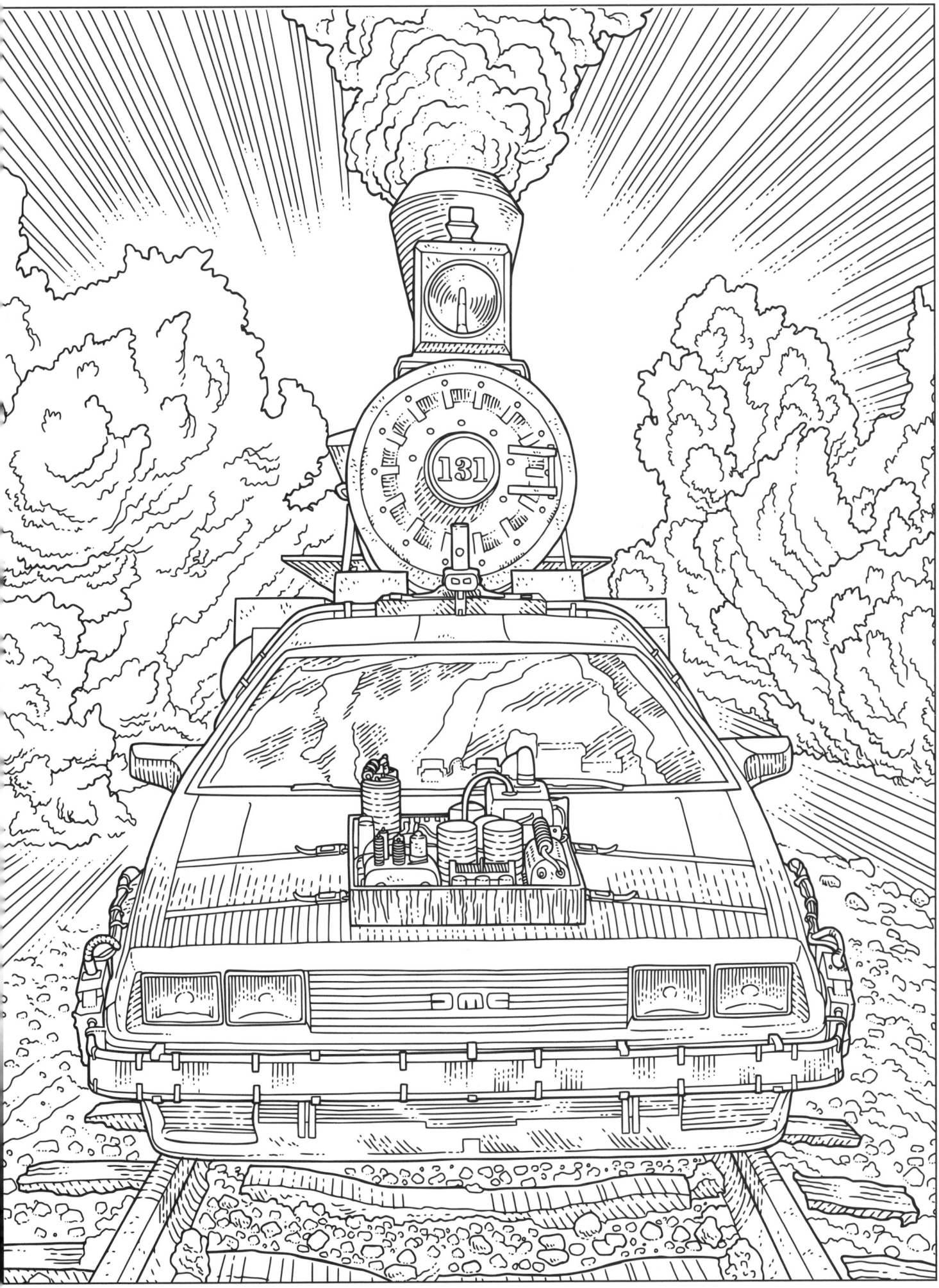
131

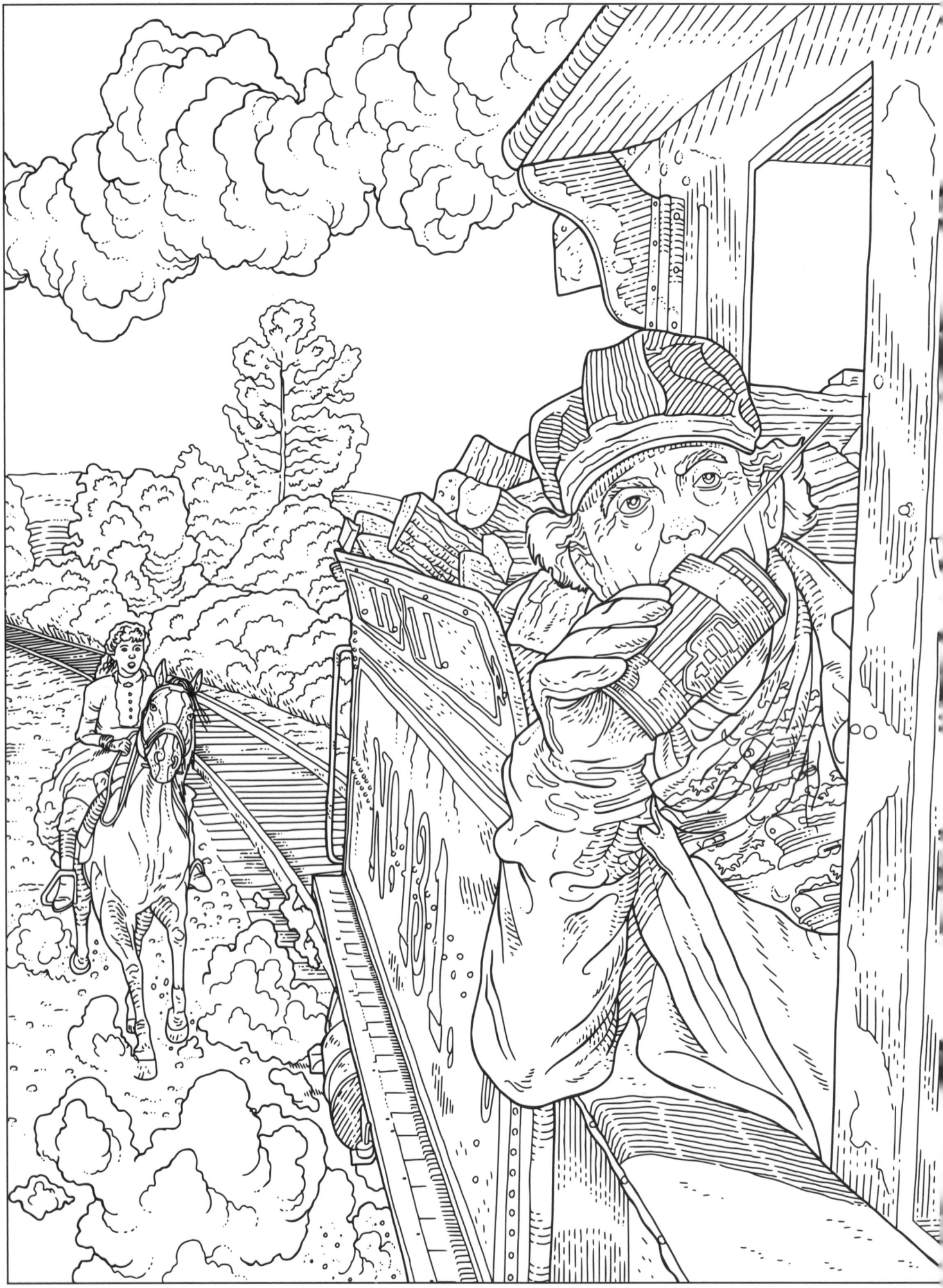

131
131

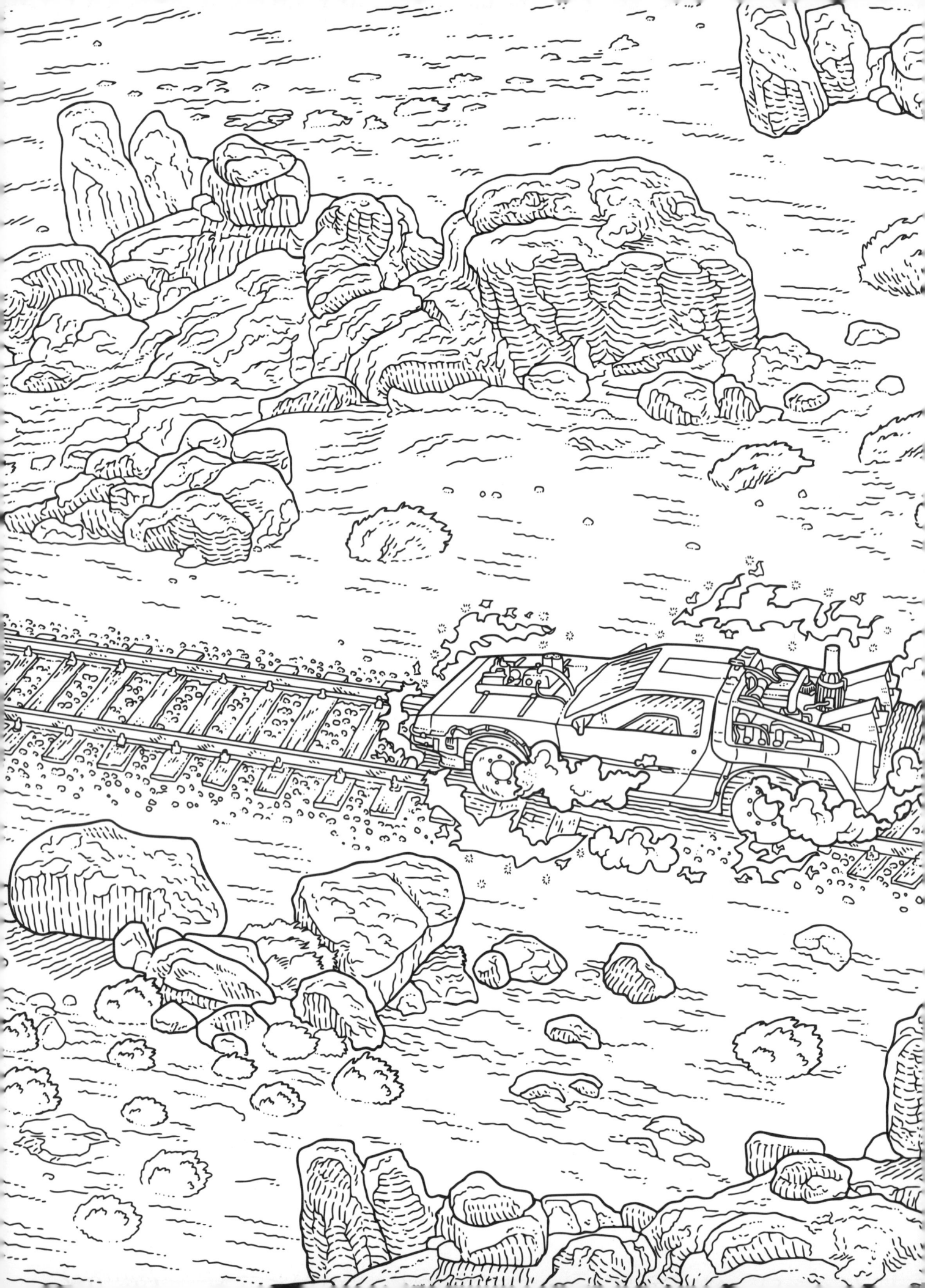

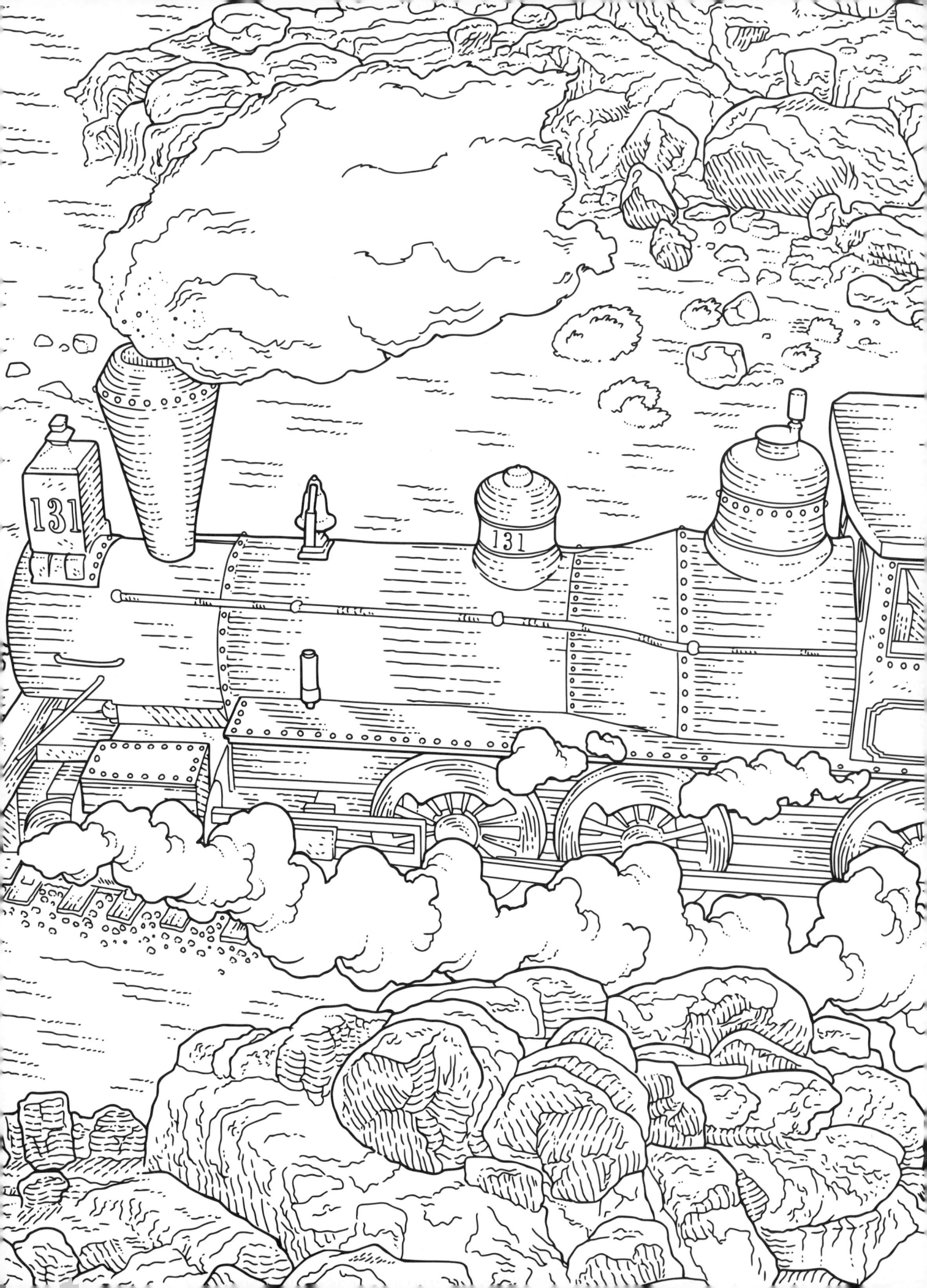
131
131

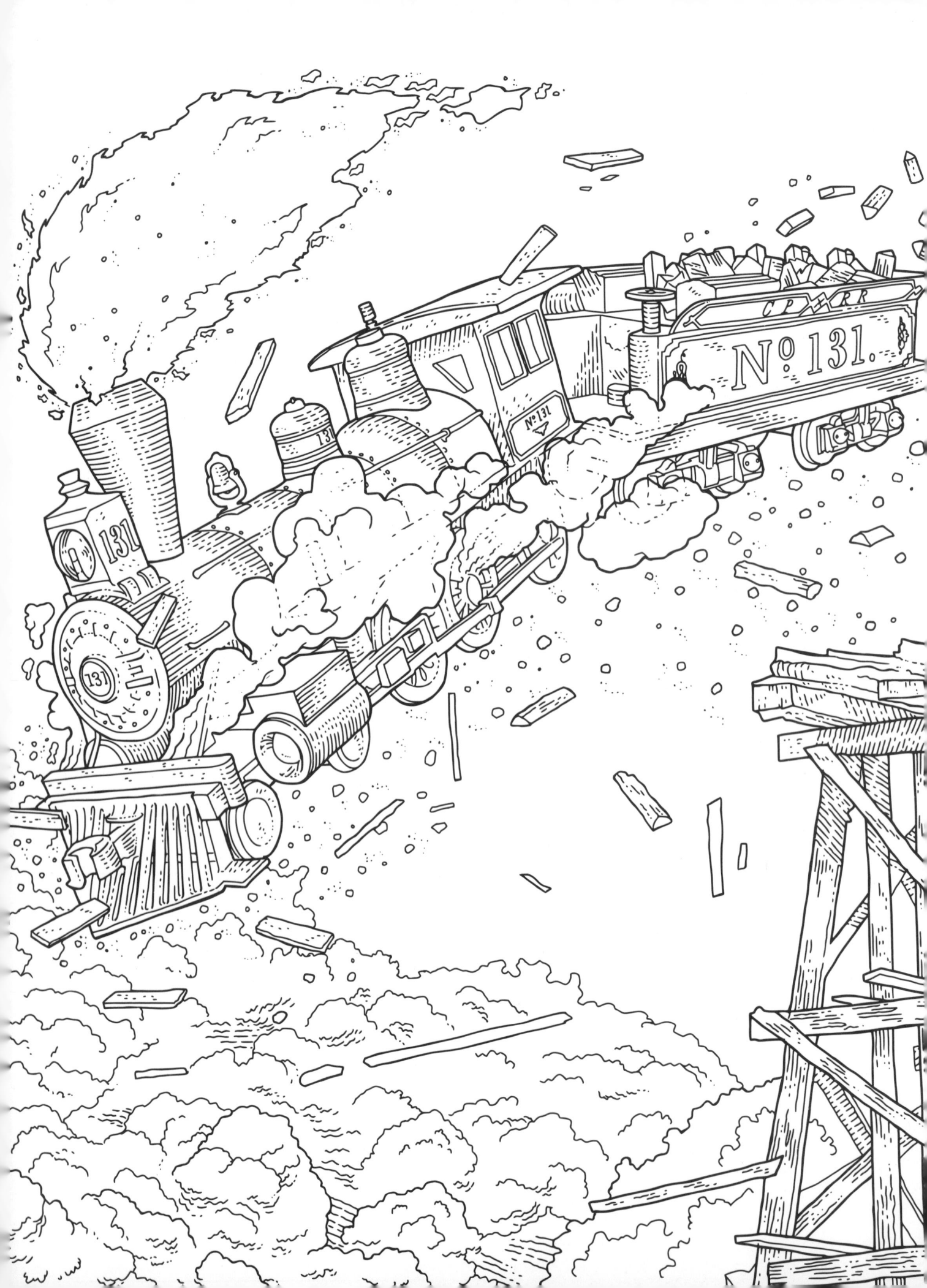
C P R R
Nº 131.
Nº 131
131
131
131

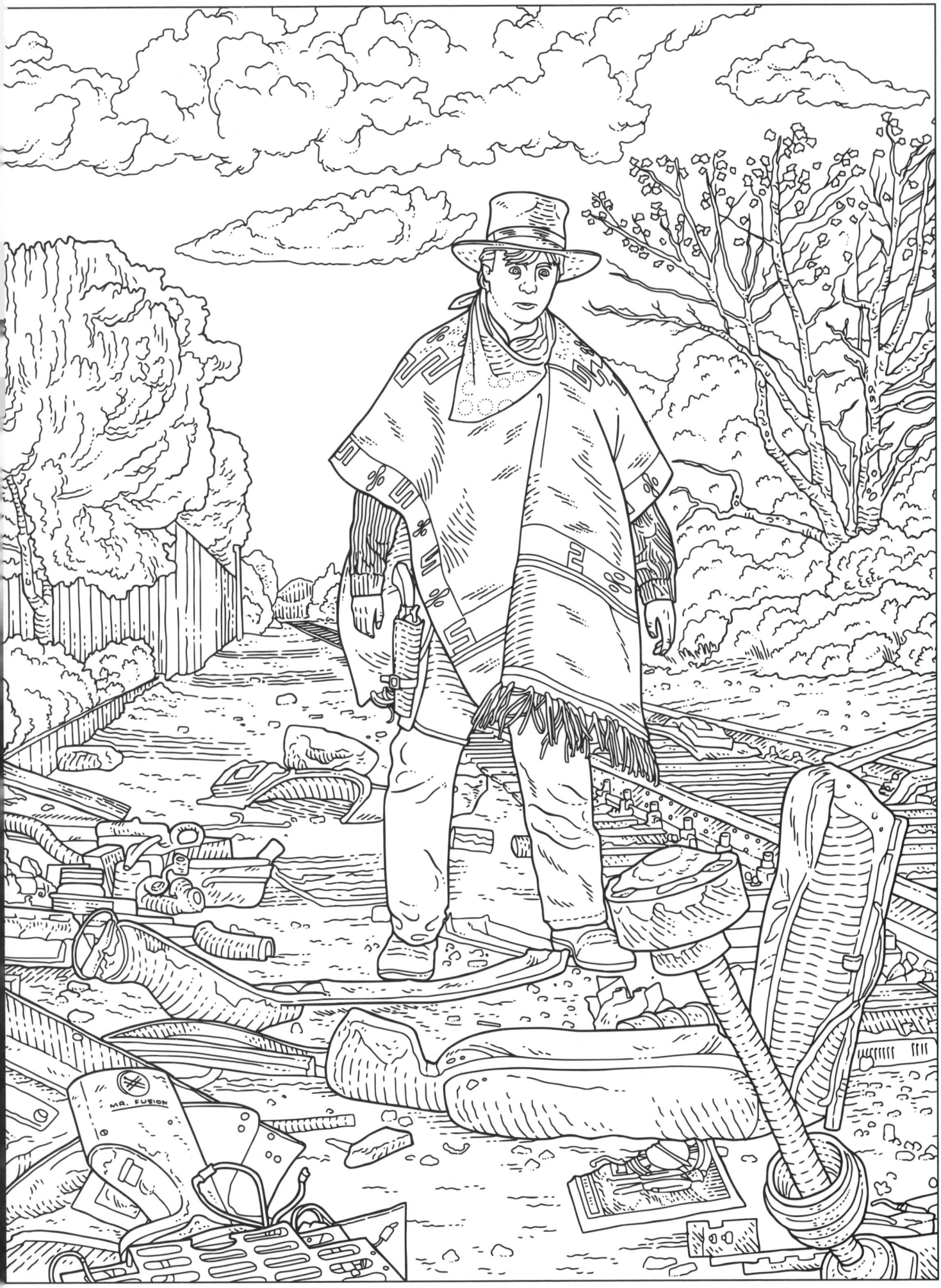
MR. FUSION

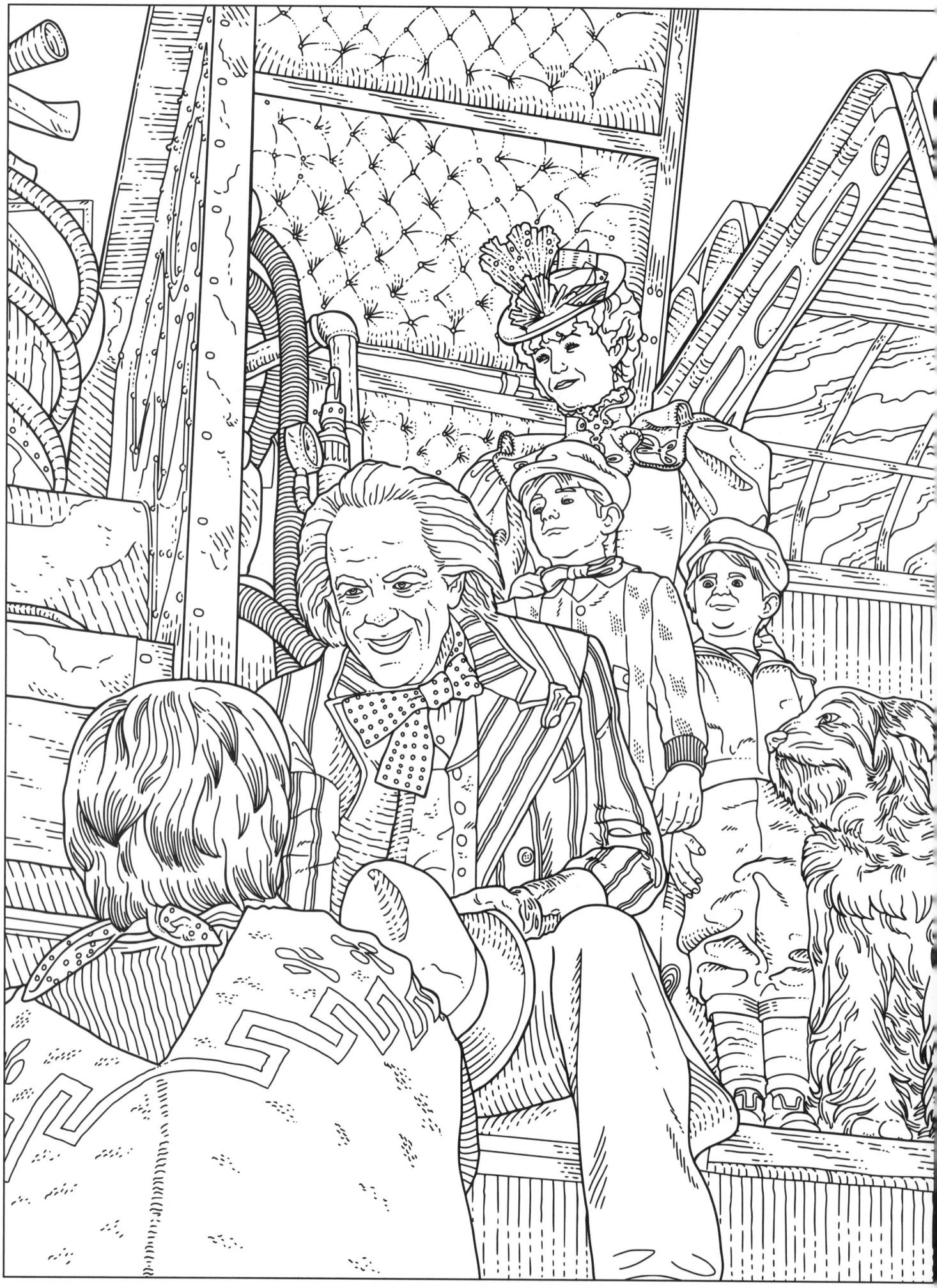

INSIGHT
EDITIONS

PO Box 3088
San Rafael, CA 94912
www.insighteditions.com

Find us on Facebook: www.facebook.com/InsightEditions
Follow us on Twitter: @insighteditions
Follow us on Instagram: @insighteditions

Copyright © 2023 Universal City Studios LLC and Amblin Entertainment, Inc.
All Rights Reserved.

All rights reserved. Published by Insight Editions, San Rafael, California, in 2023.

No part of this book may be reproduced in any form without written permission from the publisher.

ISBN: 979-8-88663-269-9

Publisher: Raoul Goff
VP, Co-Publisher: Vanessa Lopez
VP, Creative: Chrissy Kwasnik
VP, Manufacturing: Alix Nicholaeff
VP, Group Managing Editor: Vicki Jaeger
Publishing Director: Jamie Thompson
Senior Designer: Judy Wiatrek Trum
Editor: Stephen Fall
Editorial Assistant: Jennifer Pellman
Production Editor: Michael Hylton
Production Associate: Tiffani Patterson
Senior Production Manager, Subsidiary Rights: Lina s Palma-Temena

Illustrations by Valentin Ramon

ROOTS of PEACE REPLANTED PAPER

Insight Editions, in association with Roots of Peace, will plant two trees for each tree used in the manufacturing of this book. Roots of Peace is an internationally renowned humanitarian organization dedicated to eradicating land mines worldwide and converting war-torn lands into productive farms and wildlife habitats. Roots of Peace will plant two million fruit and nut trees in Afghanistan and provide farmers there with the skills and support necessary for sustainable land use.

Manufactured in China by Insight Editions

10 9 8 7 6 5 4 3 2